SQUIRRELS
at the
BIRDFEEDER

To Peggy O'Farrell

Your help on this book was invaluable and greatly appreciated.

With Admiration

11/14/2002

SQUIRRELS at the BIRDFEEDER

Taking Aim
at Politicians, CEOs,
and Other Pests

Dick Yarbrough

Cover Illustration by David Boyd

Published by Looking Glass Books
Decatur, Georgia

Manufactured in the United States of America

ISBN 1-929619-13-8

To Zachary, Brian, Nicholas, and Thomas,
and to the grandmother and children
who made them all possible.

Contents

Foreword

A dying Gov. Eugene Talmadge summoned Ralph McGill, the famous editor of *The Atlanta Constitution*, to his hospital bed and whispered.

"Ralph, I want you to write my biography, and I want you to call it *The Life of Eugene Talmadge by His Enemy Ralph McGill*. You'll make a lot of money."

That tale from the 1940s, as apocryphal as it may be, accurately illustrates the relationship between Talmadge and McGill, who was one of Talmadge's fiercest foes and, at the same time, a great admirer of his political skills.

Though Dick Yarbrough has not yet invited me to write his life's story, we have had a similar relationship—one of admiration and downright distrust.

For more than three decades, we were, to put it mildly, adversaries. Yarbrough was the king of the flacks, a public relations genius working first for Southern Bell, then BellSouth, and finally the Atlanta Committee for the Olympic Games.

His job was to show the best face possible for his clients and to hide their blemishes from public view. My job, as I saw it then and now, was to uncover the acne that surely lurked on that best possible face.

From the 1960s to the late 20th century, Dick and I played fox and hound, reporter versus flack. I'm not sure any winner emerged, because we both quit before the game was over.

I departed my job with *The Atlanta Journal-Constitution* to start a political newsletter. Yarbrough hung up his pin-striped battle fatigues to go into retirement, which didn't last long.

One day a couple of years ago, I happened to pick up a copy of the *Atlanta Business Chronicle* and discovered a column by my old artful-dodger pal, Yarbrough, writing his heart out and spilling the beans.

"The sonofabitch is finally telling the world what he never would tell me," I said to no one in particular. Yarbrough's columns were letting it all hang out. He assailed the deceptive practices of the corporate establishment for whom he had shilled. He lashed out at the political pooh-bahs for their phoniness and ineptness. He made some of his readers and all of his editors uncomfortable.

But he had a message, and he was determined to deliver it.

I phoned Yarbrough and suggested he throw in with me, and let me handle his columns. "I can not only give your work greater circulation, I can demonstrate to you what the Grady College of Mass Communications or Journalism or whatever it calls itself never could—commas and comas are different," I declared modestly.

The rest is history. We took in the wayward Yarbrough with an agreement he would write mostly about the corporate world—an agreement he quickly set aside.

He decided that instead of being the consummate tell-all company insider, he would become a comedian and social commentator. The jury is still out on both counts, but Yarbrough's columns have stimulated passionate comment and occasionally violent reaction throughout the state. Some readers have written us, saying only that Yarbrough has finally expressed The Truth. Others have phoned in bomb threats. Yarbrough doesn't hesitate to go to the heart of all matters, some of which he plainly has no knowledge. But, as this humble commentator can testify, ignorance can be a blessing to journalists, allowing them to tread bravely and without a care where learned men and women would never venture.

Read this book, and you'll see what I mean.

One other thing. Yarbrough wrote a previous tome, *And They Call Them Games*, which is, to date, the only published detailed account of the ups and downs of the 1996 Olympics in Atlanta.

Yarbrough never claimed objectivity, but he offered pages and pages of never-before-revealed information on what went wrong—and right—with the Games.

Alas, the book was not widely read. The Atlanta media mostly boycotted it, because former public-relations mastermind Yarbrough did the unthinkable. He succeeded in alienating the big newspapers with his scathing criticism of their Games' coverage. Scant reviews equal not many book sales.

I wrote a favorable piece about Yarbrough's book, suggesting someone had finally given us a real peek at the truth of the Games, and offered it to my client newspapers for possible use.

One editor wrote me a cryptic note: "We can't use this. This can't be regarded as a credible review. You and Dick have been friends for far too long."

If he only knew.

— Bill Shipp

Introduction

When I retired in 1996 after laboring four decades in the corporate vineyards, first with BellSouth and its predecessor, Southern Bell, and then with the Atlanta Committee for the Olympic Games, I was happily contemplating raising flowers and lowering my golf handicap.

Much of my career had been spent as corporate spokesman, and this often placed me in hand-to-hand combat with the news media. That I survived was a miracle. That an industry publication had named me one of the "100 Most Influential Public Relations Practitioners of the 20th Century" was a strong signal to quit while I was ahead. It was time to get out of the pressure cooker and into pruning azaleas and trying to tame a wicked slice.

Then one day in 1998, the *Atlanta Business Chronicle* called and asked me to write a guest column about the city of Atlanta two years after the Olympic Games. As you will see from the first column in this book, I didn't think much of the city's performance before, during, or after the Games, and I said so. I spared no one—the inept city government, the leaderless business community and, least of all, the Atlanta newspapers. In my opinion, they all had blown this once-in-a-lifetime opportunity.

The *Atlanta Business Chronicle* was delighted with the reaction to the column and suggested a regular stint in that highly respected publication. The pruning shears and the golf lessons would have to wait. This looked like fun.

I quickly learned that strong opinions begat even stronger reactions. I have been praised, panned, called a wild-eyed liberal, a moss-bound conservative, a redneck, and urged to "go back North where I came from." (I was born and raised in East Point, Georgia.)

My column is now syndicated through the offices of my good friend and veteran political observer, Bill Shipp. Shipp tells me that I reach over a half-million households in Georgia each week. I wish I didn't know that, because it makes me wake up at night in a cold sweat, wondering if I got all the commas in the right places.

I had been asked on numerous occasions about turning my columns into a book. I wasn't sure how to go about doing that but, fortunately, I knew someone who did. Dick Parker, a friend and successful bookmeister, agreed to undertake the mission. This required him to read all my columns and decide which were worth publication, keep me on schedule, and handle a million other details. His reward is in heaven. We were fortunate to get the hugely talented David Boyd to do the cover design, although when I insisted that he make me look like Robert Redford, he refused. That's all I need—an artist with integrity.

Lots of people are due applause for their help and support, starting with my family. The Woman Who Shares My Name has qualified for sainthood by just being under the same roof with me for 44 years. My son, Ken, and daughter, Maribeth, were smart enough to marry over their heads and then produce four grandsons named Zachary, Brian, Nicholas, and Thomas. Don't get me started on them or you won't have time to read this book. They are the light of my life.

Michelle Cobb, who is the heart and soul of Bill Shipp's operation, manages to get my column where it is supposed to be every week, on time and always with good cheer. Glen Jackson, principal in the firm of Jackson-Spalding Public Relations, and his able aide, Randall Kirsch, gave me sound advice on how to get the word out about the book, suggesting some folks just might want to buy it. Peggy O'Farrell took me high-tech, which is akin to putting a tuxedo on a pig, and created a web page for me.

Of course, none of this would be possible if not for the newspapers that allow me to state my opinions each week. I am sure there are times they flinch at some of my comments, but they let me say what is on my mind and in my heart. God bless them one and all.

Finally, a special thanks to all the overpaid professional athletes, yuppie-boomers who drive SUVs like unguided missiles, the country of France, the state of California, narrow-minded special interest groups (I think that is redundant), pompous politicians, greedy CEOs, and equally greedy squirrels for giving me ample targets at which to shoot each week. May I never miss.

— *Dick Yarbrough*

SQUIRRELS
at the
BIRDFEEDER

Dying Atlanta
May Not Be
Worth Saving

June 26, 1998

Permit me a bit of heresy.

Atlanta is on an inexorable descent with no one and nothing to stop it—and here's the heresy part—I'm not sure it really matters.

I reached this radical conclusion during my tenure at the Atlanta Committee for the Olympic Games. The city had a chance to put itself among the great cities of the world and blew it.

Atlanta, like the braggart whose bluff is called, couldn't deliver when the time came.

When Billy Payne pulled off his miracle, the city was presented a golden opportunity. Rather than cooperate, the city government's response was to squeeze the Olympic planners for every dollar they could, play the race card at every opportunity, and then attempt to ambush our own Olympic partners by offering sponsorships to competitors.

This in spite of the fact that the 1996 Olympic Games were privately financed and that Atlanta was indemnified from any financial responsibility.

What we were left with was the enduring legacy of Mayor Bill Campbell's buddy, Munson Steed, and the ill-fated vending program that was an international embarrassment.

Sadly, everyone else—media, business, civic leaders—stood around and watched the city make a fool of itself on the world stage. It took the Olympic Games to show our weakness to the world—and to ourselves. We are better at "talking the talk" than "walking the walk."

If we can allow ourselves to be brutally honest, the city of Atlanta's problems are serious; no amount of boosterism will change that. This city is dying before our eyes.

Our sewer system is antiquated. Our water is dirty. Our air is foul. Our downtown is moribund. Underground Atlanta is in danger of folding (again). It is hard to walk the streets in the daytime and not be accosted by panhandlers.

Special interest groups intent on maintaining status quo have the government by the throat. The most efficient and effective bureaucrat in the city, airport director Angela Gittens, is gone. (The only positive recent development in the city is Centennial Olympic Park, and that, like the Olympic Games, was the brainchild of Billy Payne, not the city.)

What is needed desperately is a catalyst. The Olympic Games didn't do it, and I do not see a candidate on the horizon. In some cities, the media serve that role, but our local daily had minimal influence among the inner city citizens it purports to represent, and certainly has none with the mayor.

I don't see that role in the business community, either. The days of those who worked for the betterment of Atlanta simply because they loved the city are gone.

They have been replaced by CEOs who are international in their focus. BellSouth Corp. (my alma mater), The Coca-Cola Co., Delta Air Lines Inc., United Parcel Service Inc., Georgia-Pacific Corp., and Southern Co. don't have the same focus on Atlanta as did their predecessors. (Pete Correll is making an effort, but his focus is on regional traffic problems, not just downtown.)

This is not meant to be criticism. Business is not about social responsibility; it is first about returning a profit to its owners, and, today, international expansion clearly outweighs concerns about quality of life in Atlanta. (The one exception would be Southern Co.'s CEO, Bill Dahlberg, who just might have the desire to effect some fundamental changes. He certainly has the ability.)

The Atlanta Convention & Visitors Bureau and Central Atlanta Progress have minimal ability to pressure the city into change, and the Metro Atlanta Chamber of Commerce is influential only because of its very able leader, Sam Williams. Add to the dilemma this interesting comment from a close friend of the mayor: When I asked who in the business community Bill Campbell listened to, he replied, "Nobody. Business doesn't deliver votes."

Even if someone is willing to try and halt the slide, there are huge risks. The rights of the homeless are vigorously defended, even if it lessens the quality of life for the rest of us. The concerned black clergy can paralyze city government with calls for action from the pulpit and can paralyze business by shouting racism at any efforts to change the status quo.

But do we really need the city of Atlanta? Not as much as the city needs the rest of us. The region has no natural boundaries, so we can grow in any direction and, as our traffic patterns will attest, we have.

We don't have to come downtown and won't. Business will come to us, whether we are in Cherokee, Bartow, Paulding, Henry, or any other more distant counties. We can shop in bright, clean megamalls, eat at a growing number of fine restaurants, work in nearby business parks, and leave the city to those who can least afford it—the poor.

Given what has happened to the city of Atlanta, we can't even lay claim to being "The Next Great City." That honor, unfortunately, belongs to Charlotte, which took the title along with our banks.

This Is
About Caring,
Not Racism

This is not the column I intended to write.

My first column on the current situation in Atlanta understandably brought a huge amount of reaction. An overwhelming number of people that I heard from were in complete agreement with my views. With the exception of my good friend and Bill Campbell confidant, Steve Labovitz, those left to defend the city either couldn't mount a truthful defense or figured it didn't matter what I said as long as nothing changed the status quo.

A number of people called and wrote to ask what could be done to salvage this sinking ship. This column was intended to offer some positive suggestions on that point.

As I was putting the finishing touches to that effort, I read of the Metro Group's concerns about the impending water privatization bids and the reaction of City Hall to their concerns. The incident provided a perfect example of what is wrong with this city.

Under the leadership of noted Atlanta architect George Heery, 35 prominent Atlantans who make up the Metro Group, an independent watchdog group, had questions about some of the procedures and processes of bidding for Atlanta's notoriously bad water system.

This was a $500 million to $600 million project, the largest water privatization in the country. They were doing what any good business person would do—ask tough questions.

What was City Hall's reaction to their concerns? The mayor said they were "irresponsible," "outrageous," "misguided," "politically motivated." This to a group that, in addition to Heery, includes attorney Jimmy Sibley; the Atlanta Regional Commission's Harry West; former mayors Andy Young and Sam Massell; Walter Hundley, who was Campbell's director of the Atlanta Economic Development Council and Inman Allen, chairman of Ivan Allen Co.

Then, the mayor and his mouthpiece, Jibari Simama, pulled

out the race card and accused the group of "attempting to discredit African-American leadership" and of a "surreptitious attack on the city's minority participation program."

Respectfully disagree with the mayor on anything and you're automatically a racist. This is why Atlanta is dying. Why try to make the city a better place when you are sure to be tarred with racial epithets? Who needs the hassle?

No, Mr. Mayor. These people are not racists. They are people who love Atlanta and want to see it better than it is. They want results and see enough evidence of poor management by the city with an undermanned and demoralized police force, the disgusting mess around the Five Points MARTA station, an Empowerment Zone that has reaped no benefits since its creation, and an administration that doesn't return phone calls (including theirs), to have some legitimate concerns.

When you are firmly ensconced in Al Gore's cabinet (if he is elected) or some silk-stocking law firm (if he isn't), they will be living with this decision. They've got a right to ask.

Before either you or Mr. Simama were old enough to tie your shoes, Jimmy Sibley's father, John A. Sibley, was stumping this state determined to keep Georgia's public schools open when a lot of influential white racists intended to close them to black children.

Mr. Sibley's efforts were far more courageous than anything I have seen come out of City Hall. Mr. Sibley and Inman Allen's father, Mayor Ivan Allen Jr., had one important trait that is sadly missing in this City Hall. They were color-blind. To impugn the integrity and motives of these distinguished families and the other members of the Metro Group because they are concerned about a proven track record of mismanagement is unconscionable.

When I said the city was dying, I didn't know the mayor would provide such irrefutable evidence in such short order. Despite his mean-spirited diatribes, I know the Metro Group will continue to ask the hard questions.

It is going to take the collective efforts of these people and others if we were going to save the city from itself and from those who refuse to believe it is broken.

But be forewarned. It won't be easy, and you already know the thanks you can expect.

CEO Must
Take the Rap
for Poor Service
April 23, 1999

I recently had separate encounters with two Atlanta-based companies. One involved a $1600 expenditure; the other, $2.78.

Last week, I made a speech in St. Petersburg, Florida, and took my wife with me. We flew on Delta Air Lines round trip and remarked that no one seemed particularly glad to see us. Everything was perfunctory.

On the return trip, we were not even treated to the routine "Thank you for flying Delta" as we exited. As a matter of fact, the flight attendants were standing in the galley, arms folded. I could only surmise that, given the flight crew was "Salt Lake City-based," they wanted to be home working on that joyous event, the 2002 Olympic Games.

Two days later, I found myself in need of some small bolts for a rare do-it-yourself project. I went to Home Depot and asked a clerk where such items would be located. Instead of telling me, he stopped his current task of stocking shelves, took me to the correct aisle and proceeded to help me select the right size bolts, nuts and washers.

You are already ahead of me on this one. The Delta trip was the $1,600 expenditure. The Home Depot trip cost me $2.78. I was, to say the least, struck by the difference in attitude of the two companies.

This is nothing new. The Delta flight was actually more pleasant by far than most I have been on during the past several years. The Home Depot visit was typical of most of my visits there. (My only complaint is that they should stock their shelves after working hours. Those beeping tractors used to reach high shelves are dangerous and annoying.)

I can think of no business more cut-throat than the airline and retail industries. Yet, one company (Delta) seems to have lost its way. The other (Home Depot) is thriving, growing and prospering.

So what is my point? It is that the blame—and credit—falls on the shoulders of one person, the CEO. Home Depot has long stressed customer service and walked the talk. Executives Bernie

Marcus and Arthur Blank (who is CEO) have put on those garish orange aprons and actually dealt with living, breathing customers.

The daughter of a friend of mine is an attorney at Home Depot and will be required to work in one of the stores as a part of her job. Clearly, the company's focus is on the customer. That is how Home Depot makes money and they never seem to forget it.

Contrast that with Delta Air Lines. I don't believe I recall seeing Leo Mullin, Delta's CEO, working a reservations desk or taking up tickets at the gate.

In fact, I have never seen him in a center seat in coach, trying to get his bag in the little overhead bins or under the seats that have no leg room, before partaking of that god-awful Sky Deli. At Delta, profitability seems to come first, and it seems to be at the customer's expense.

CEO's have one responsibility and one only—pleasing the customer, period.

All the other things they fret over—profitability, share price, competition, business plans—are secondary to pleasing their customers. In fact, I contend that putting the customer first makes all these other responsibilities easier to manage.

All CEOs espouse good customer service as their number one priority in their annual meeting spiels. But that is just so much bull hockey. Most of them are so insulated and isolated from customers by their palace guard that they rarely ever see, or talk to a customer.

Frankly, they prefer it that way because the customer will tell them the unvarnished truth about what kind of job their company is doing and it probably will be discomfiting to them. They would rather be behind their desk, approving new cost-cutting measures such as replacing expensive employees with those maddening "punch-one-if-you live-in-Cleveland-punch-two-if-you-don't" automated machines.

That saves money. It irritates and angers the customer but it does save money.

So, if you are a CEO, or would like to be, get out and spend time—lots of time—with your customers. Ask them how you are doing and how the company is doing. You just might learn something.

You also might see Leo Mullin serving new and improved Sky Delis in coach.

Metro Group Is a Conscience for City Hall

May 28, 1999

Last week, the folks at City Hall got their undies in a wad because their mortal enemy, the Metro Group, said the city payroll is bloated and that by cutting out some of the fat, Atlanta could fund pay raises for both police and firefighters with the savings.

The mayor's pit bull, Jabari Simama, did what you would expect him to do—attacked the messenger, not the message.

His boss, Mayor Bill Campbell, has told me he has never met with the Metro Group, will never meet with them and won't allow anyone on his staff to meet with them. He and Simama have declared the group (surprise) racists and a tool of a former mayoral candidate, whom I assume to be Marvin Arrington.

I asked the group's founder and chairman, architect George Heery, why the vehemence. Heery says he doesn't know, except the mayor doesn't seem to like anybody looking over his shoulder while he does business. A city council member has said there is no deal in the city of Atlanta that doesn't have the potential for cronyism, which means somebody had better be looking. That group is the Metro Group.

Heery doesn't necessarily agree with me, but I think the business community is too worried about Atlanta's image to put the screws to the city and demand it operate efficiently and honestly. That leaves the Metro Group staked out in a lonely but critically-important place as the only credible watchdog in Atlanta. It damn sure ain't the media.

How could an organization made up of the Sibley family, the Allen family, former Council member Myrtle Davis, Georgia Research Alliance head Bill Todd, former Atlanta Economic Development Walter Huntley, former mayor Sam Massell, civic leader Bob Silverman and others be racists? They are not. To insult them as tools of Marvin Arrington is laughable and regrettable. As a matter of fact, Heery says before the last election, the Metro Group was split about evenly between the candidates.

On the good news side, the Metro Group has had some success with the Atlanta School Board, which accepted their help, and the Metro Group also was instrumental in putting the city's water system contract bidding process under scrutiny, saving the city some $200 million over the next 20 years, according to Heery. (Incidentally, the water system was not privatized. It is still owned by the city but turned over to a private company to operate.)

Heery is absolutely bullish on Gov. Roy Barnes' focus on regional solutions to the water quality, air quality and traffic issues and sees a future of regional authorities for cities and counties without the will to consolidate. If Georgia legislators can summon the political resolve of Gov. Barnes, they may be able to consolidate police departments, fire departments, water departments, etc. and rid us of duplication. If so, they will have a strong ally in the Metro Group.

I asked Heery why he started the Metro Group in the first place and why he absorbs the diatribes of City Hall. In the early '90s, he and Johnnetta Cole, then president of Spelman College, decided that the Atlanta School Board was injecting race into everything, and a biracial commission was needed to step in and offer solutions. Thus, the Metro Group was born and quickly discovered that the problems of the school board permeate City Hall as well.

Now, eight years later, Heery's thanks is unprofessional abuse from City Hall and a passive business community. Where is the reward? Heery says the people who stop him on the sidewalk and say "thank you" for caring enough about Atlanta to keep the current administration under a spotlight is reward enough.

So, thank you, George Heery and the Metro Group. Keep the light shining.

Coke's Crisis Stems from Corporate Culture

July 15, 1999

I am a great admirer of The Coca-Cola Company. I own stock in the company and have no plans to sell it.

Having said that, I am not surprised that Coca-Cola finds itself in deep trouble in Europe. It has to do with their culture.

If you think about it, Coca-Cola sells sugared water. That's all. Just sugared water. Yet, they have managed to do it so skillfully for so long that the company has taken on an almost mystical aura, even to its employees.

Its success is due to a corporate culture that is one part superior marketing (How else can you sell sugared water all over the world?) and one part junkyard dog lawyering. Coca-Cola lawyers are among the most aggressive in the world, enforcing the company's rules on how and where Coca-Cola is sold. They take no prisoners. This combination of marketing and legal muscle has made the company extraordinarily successful and perhaps feeling a tad omnipotent.

Enter the dustup in Belgium and France over supposedly contaminated Coca-Cola products. The company's culture didn't allow it to respond as quickly as it should have and the result was a crisis. Experience has taught me that crisis situations have two factors. First, a crisis is a crisis because it is out of your control. Second, a company will react to an external crisis based on how it normally does business. If the company is run by lawyers, then the lawyers will manage the crisis. If run by engineers (God forbid!) then engineers will come to the fore in a crisis. The culture is determined by how the CEO wants the company to run. Doug Ivester, Coca-Cola's CEO, is a numbers man, and a good one, but like most people who come up through the accounting ranks, not someone who inherently understands the illogic of the external environment, which will bite you in the butt at anytime no matter how omnipotent you think you are.

That is why I had to chuckle at the news reports that Ivester had called Jim Burke, retired CEO of Johnson & Johnson, for advice. Burke, you will remember, is the genius behind the handling of the Tylenol crisis some years ago. But to compare Coca-Cola's culture with J&J is like comparing butter to butterfly. At Johnson & Johnson, public relations was as important to Burke as was his marketing department. Thus, when the Tylenol crisis occurred, the natural reaction of J&J was to think externally first, everything else second. As a result, what could have been an embarrassment and blemish to the company turned out to be their finest hour and an hour that other companies, including Coca-Cola, have been trying with little or no success to emulate ever since.

Coca-Cola is now doing the right things but much more slowly than they should have. Their mea culpas sound more like a strategic ploy than an honest apology. Certainly not like the dynamic chairman of Chrysler, Lee Iaacoca, who found out that his company had been turning back the odometers of executives' cars and selling them as new. Against the advice of his lawyers, he quickly ran full-page ads saying "We Goofed" and pledging nothing like that would ever happen again while he was chairman. Now that is an apology.

And don't forget Don Keough's superb handling of the New Coke debacle back in the mid-'80s. I suspect had Keough been on the job at Coca-Cola this time, the response to the issues in Europe would have been much quicker and more decisive. He was an anomaly in The Coca-Cola Company—a great marketer who also understood the external environment.

Like most crises, this too shall pass. As soon as the EU has finished harumphing and Belgium and France have exacted their pound of flesh from the company's hide, things will slowly get back to normal and the world will move on to other matters.

But if the company is as smart as I think they are, they will remember this ordeal and empower their public relations people to identify and deal with future crises and let the marketing people and the lawyers stick with selling the sugared water.

Black Demagogues Replace White Dimwits

November 5, 1999

For the life of me, I can't understand why people like Bill Campbell, Billy McKinney, Tyrone Brooks and all the other Al Sharpton wannabes don't emulate the example of Andrew Young, former mayor of Atlanta, former ambassador to the United Nations and a great human being.

Unlike the aforementioned crowd who do nothing but talk the talk (incessantly), Andrew Young has walked the walk. He was on the front lines of the civil rights movement as chief lieutenant to Dr. Martin Luther King Jr. and endured more bad days than Campbell, McKinney, Brooks et al. combined. Yet, he came out the other side of that battle as a man that, befitting his standing as a minister, long ago forgave those of us who were insensitive to people's worth because of the color of their skin.

I spent some memorable hours with Andy Young while I was with the Atlanta Committee for the Olympic Games. I was the managing director of communications and he was co-chairman of the board. Sometimes, he would drop by the office to chat and sometimes with an observation or suggestion for me. In the process, I got to know up close a man I had long admired from afar. The thing that impressed me most about Andy is his compassion for other people. He is at home with kings and paupers, executives and laborers, sports figures and peanut vendors, the richest of the rich, the poorest of the poor and he cares for them all. To walk through an airport with him—any airport—is an experience you won't soon forget. He is easily one of the most recognizable people on the planet and one of the least affected by his fame.

If you can get him to talk about his experiences in the civil rights movement, you get a sense of just how brave a man he was and yet how modest he is in the retelling of those days. Much of what he shared with me I consider to be private conversations, including some wonderful stories that prove even in the darkest of times, he never lost his sense of humor.

Looking back on those moments, I wish I had asked him if he was frustrated at seeing what has happened to the City of Atlanta. Is he embarrassed that a group of people displays the kind of prejudice that he fought to overcome? How does he feel about local politicians screaming race every time something threatens their power base? Is he sad that today we have a reversal of what he found in Atlanta in the early '60s? Instead of the white supremacist dimwits who preached about the inferiority of blacks, now we have black demagogues spouting racial epithets every bit as prejudiced as we once heard from the J.B. Stoners of the world.

I don't think this is what Andrew Young risked his life for—to perpetuate a bunch of second-rate politicians who couldn't get elected dog catcher without shutting out and shouting down anyone who dares disagree with them.

While he was mayor, Andrew Young reached out to everybody in the city, black and white. I am amazed the current mayor doesn't see this. He is a lot of things—mean-spirited, thin-skinned and arrogant—but he isn't dumb. The same with McKinney and Brooks and those of their ilk. Why don't they model themselves after the style and class of Andrew Young?

The answer is easy. None of them can. They aren't politically astute enough to understand that they could have even more power—the thing they all crave—if they only reached out and brought others into their tent. They are afraid that if they do, right-minded people will see them for what they are and kick their butts out of office.

Thankfully, this was not Andrew Young's character and he will be fondly remembered when the rest of this crowd is an embarrassing footnote on the pages of Atlanta's history.

I have had this great man on my mind since I heard he will soon undergo prostate cancer surgery. Having suffered the same situation myself a few years ago, I know what he is going through and I pray for his speedy recovery. The prognosis seems positive and that is encouraging because his work isn't yet done. He still has promises to keep and miles to go before he sleeps.

I wish to God there were more like him.

Nothing Special About Caray Except Poorly Concealed Contempt

I usually leave sports matters to the experts but I must take exception to a recent column by my longtime friend and colleague, Dick Williams, professing admiration for the rude and boorish behavior of Atlanta Braves broadcaster Skip Caray. I rise to defend the good and decent people who call into his show, only to be insulted, ridiculed and intimidated by a guy who sounds like he would rather be doing anything than talking to (ugh!) common people. The only one who comes close to Skip Caray in barely disguised disdain for the fans is Georgia football coach Jim Donnan, who needs to be reminded of the necessity to beat Tennessee, Florida and Tech a few times before he gets as arrogant as he sounds.

Assuming he is getting paid to flip off baseball fans nightly, Caray should back up to collect his paycheck. In fact, there is nothing special about him except his poorly concealed contempt for his callers. He is just another of the local "homers" that populate our airwaves in Atlanta—men and women who gush and fawn over our underachieving professional sports teams and forget the fans who are at the mercy of the high prices and poor performance so much a part of our local sports landscape.

Caray reserves his bad attitude for those who are forced to pay usurious prices for tickets, bottled water and the like only to be disappointed year after year. His contempt needs to be directed at the organization that pays him for its continued inability to win the big one. But, bad attitude aside, he isn't the worst of the broadcasting homers in Atlanta. The leading candidate has to be Atlanta Hawks and WSB Radio sportscaster Steve Holman. With new Hawk addition J.R. Rider missing from the team and, at the time, his whereabouts unknown, I listened to Holman lob nerf ball questions at Hawks coach Lenny Wilkins about the beautiful dressing rooms at Philips Arena. No questions about Rider, who will likely go down as the Hawks' worst acquisition ever. (A good question might have been, "Lenny, the dressing rooms are nice. How many nights do you think J.R. Rider will be in them this year? Five times? Six, maybe?")

I know New York is a rather sensitive subject for Braves fans, but I was there during the National League Championship Series after Ricky Henderson had overrun third base and had cost the Mets a critical run. The local sportscasters ripped Henderson and Manager Bobby Valentine for dumb baseball and for the lame excuses as to why it happened. It was brutal. But it was no doubt the way most Mets fans felt. Contrast that with the kid-glove treatment given Braves manager Bobby Cox by Atlanta's sportscasters, including Caray. I dare say that is not the way most Braves fans feel about Cox, who has given new meaning to the term "second place." No wonder underachievers enjoy playing in Atlanta!

As meek as Atlanta's sportscasters are, there is one notable exception. The man who should be the role model for all of the fawning homers in town is Atlanta Falcons radio analyst and long-time player, Jeff Van Note. If the Falcons make a good play—a rare occurrence these days—he says so. They screw up and Van Note will let you know that, too. And he will let you know who was responsible and why. He is clearly the most credible sports voice in Atlanta. There is no way he would let Bobby Cox and Lenny Wilkens off the hook like the sycophants associated with the Braves and Hawks.

One last word on Skip Caray. He does have one redeeming virtue that should be duly noted. His son, Chip, currently the Chicago Cubs broadcaster, is one of the finest young men I have met. He is friendly, gracious, and seems totally unaffected by the fact that he has such a prestigious job at such a young age. A job, incidentally, that once belonged to his grandfather, Harry Caray. Before his career is over, he will be considered one of the best ever. Mark my words.

I couldn't conceive of young Chip Caray acting like such a jerk while dealing with baseball fans. I believe he appreciates the game of baseball too much and understands from whence the support for the game comes.

If there is a Caray to admire and write about, it is Chip, not his old man.

I Think That I
Shall Never See
Another Dr. Cook

December 17, 1999

In an earlier column, I alluded to a reunion prompted by sportswriter Mitch Albom's book, *Tuesdays With Morrie*, in which a disillusioned sportswriter hunts up his professor, Morrie Schwartz, who is dying of Lou Gehrig's disease. Rather than comforting his professor on his regular Tuesday visits, Albom ends up having his own outlook changed by the wisdom of his mentor. It is a remarkable story.

The more I read, the more uncomfortable I became because I, too, had a professor who made an enormous difference in my life. For a number of years I told myself I should find him and thank him for what he had meant to me. *Tuesdays With Morrie* made me do that.

My "Morrie" is Dr. Raymond A. Cook, retired professor emeritus of English at Valdosta State University and former president of Young Harris College. More important, he was an English professor at Georgia State in the late '50s when I was a sophomore there. I was on academic probation and in danger of flunking out of school. My buddies had quit and had gotten jobs. It seemed just a matter of time perhaps until the same fate would befall me. At that critical point I ended up in an English Literature class taught by Dr. Cook.

Two things happened in that class that changed my life. First was the way he taught. He would begin reading poetry from the textbook and without missing a beat, would close the book, lean back, and focus on some distant point as he continued to recite. I found myself mesmerized as I listened to him. His obvious passion for the written word connected with me. It got me interested in the class and in school and in doing better work. Then one fateful day, Dr. Cook asked someone to analyze "Trees" by Joyce Kilmer. Much-inspired by now, I volunteered and proclaimed it one of the world's great poems. Big mistake. (Trust me on this one—"Trees" is a poorly-constructed poem, as I was to find out.)

Even these many years later, I can remember the scowl on the face of this kind and gentle man. He proceeded to dress me down in front of the class for not having taken the time to properly study the poem and for not knowing what I was talking about. "Mr. Yarbrough," he said sternly, "Always think before you speak!"

Lesson learned and never forgotten. Many times in my career I was impatient to interrupt a serious discussion with my opinion when Dr. Cook's admonition would come to mind. "Think first." It probably saved my job more than once!

Whatever I have accomplished in life has been the result of good and wise people who were there at critical junctures in my life. Dr. Raymond Cook is one of those people. I went to see him in Valdosta to thank him for keeping me in college and for teaching me to think first and talk later. He didn't remember me but he was delighted that I would take the time and make the effort to look him up and tell him of his impact on my life.

Out of that visit has come a wonderful friendship. We correspond regularly through e-mail. He is a spry and vigorous 80 years old, a collector of antique Rolls Royce automobiles, a ham radio operator, and an authority on Georgia poet Byron Herbert Reece. I count myself fortunate to have this Renaissance Man as my friend.

I don't know who was the greatest beneficiary of our meeting, him for having inspired me to finish college or me for having let him know what an influence he had on me. But it doesn't really matter.

What matters is that all of us have a Morrie Schwartz or a Raymond Cook in our past—a high school teacher or college professor or coach who inspired us to do better or to be better and because of them, we did. Chances are they don't know it because we have never told them. It took me four decades to get around to telling Dr. Cook.

Do yourself a favor. Write or call and say "thank you for making a difference in my life." No gift you get or give this holiday season will come close to the joy and satisfaction you will receive from such a gesture. I know.

So thank you for what you did for me, Dr. Cook. And thank you, Mitch Albom, for inspiring me to find him. And a special thanks to Joyce Kilmer, wherever you are.

To My Grandsons: Learn from My Time's Mistakes

To: Zachary and Nicholas Wansley; Brian and Thomas Yarbrough

As you read this, the 20th century is history. The new one belongs to you, my beloved grandsons. I hope you won't repeat the same mistakes my generation made. To that end, permit me some observations that may be of help as you make your way into the unknown.

I grew up when World War III—the ultimate war—hovered over us like a dark cloud. That threat is gone but, unfortunately, it looks like you are going to have to live with constant risk of terrorism and perhaps an eroding of our individual freedoms to combat it. So, you start this century with a different kind of uncertainty. Speaking of war, I saw what the Vietnam War, along with the assassinations of John and Robert Kennedy and Martin Luther King did to destroy our innocence. When I look at the shameful behavior of our current president and our former Speaker of the House and the lack of outrage over their behavior, I think my generation just doesn't give a damn anymore. I hope you guys will be passionate about what is right and what isn't.

We have done extraordinary things in the 20th century. We fly higher and faster. We carry mini-computers in our pockets. We have an endless amount of information at our fingertips and we can communicate— or miscommunicate—instantly. But we seem to have gotten meaner (just listen to talk radio), more self-absorbed (just watch television) and more willing to blame others for our problems (just read the newspapers, particularly the sports sections).

When I was your age, segregation was a way of life in the South. It was a terrible injustice fomented by white racists who lived in fear of blacks getting their Constitutionally-guaranteed right to vote. When this happened, the rednecks knew they would lose power.

Today you are seeing just the opposite of what I witnessed. Now we have black racists who fear losing power to whites. Where I once heard white politicians rail about "segregation forever," today black politicians talk about "fights to the death" and "hating" those who disagree with them. So racism is still around. It is just the players who have changed. Observing your natural relationships with friends of varied backgrounds tells me that your generation may overcome the biases of our generation. I pray that will be the case. The 21st century should have no place for bigots—black or white.

Don't think it is going to be easy for people to get along. Look at the Serbs and Croats. They all look the same to me. But they know the difference and, as a result, have been killing each other for much of this millennium. Can we overcome prejudice? If we are all to survive as a nation, we will have to do better than we are doing now. A good place to start would be getting rid of the hyphen. We don't need to identify ourselves as African-Americans, Mexican-Americans, Italian-Americans, Japanese-Americans, etc. The more we do that, the more that we inalterably subordinate our own national interest. We should all be proud of our heritage. But remember, we are all Americans first, hyphens notwithstanding.

Work at developing a sense of humor. We can't laugh at ourselves anymore for fear of offending some special interest group. What passes for humor on television is either mean-spirited and directed at inept politicians or is better left in the nearest gutter. It just isn't funny.

Don't accept as gospel the news reporting of the general media in the country. They have lost touch with the public, are distrusted as an institution, and have such a liberal bias that they rarely bother to hide it anymore. Besides, I expect in the future you will get most of your news on the Internet, although I'm not sure I am comfortable with that.

By the time you are my age, you will be in the minority. You will face a host of issues that my generation did not have to deal with and some probably of our own doing. Call it getting even.

But nothing or no one will be able to disadvantage you as long as you have a good education, integrity, a strong faith and a sense of self-worth. Your parents have done a terrific job of preparing you for the journey to come.

I wish I could be around to see how well you do.

Love,

Pa

Murders and
Finger Pointing
Could Kill Buckhead

The recent murders in Buckhead, Atlanta's trendiest neighborhood, exposed one of the city's major weaknesses—a lack of leadership in the business community.

To refresh our collective memories, there have been three murders in two weeks in Buckhead, including the slaying of two persons in the wee hours following the Super Bowl. In that altercation, police arrested and are holding NFL star Ray Lewis. An investigation is ongoing for other participants.

Predictably, the incident has triggered a lot of finger pointing. Local Buckhead merchants, led by the good and able Sam Massell, Atlanta's former mayor, blame the bars for an unwillingness to control their patrons and an insistence that they stay open as late as 4 A.M. The bars complain that there should be more police available in the area. The manager of Cobalt Lounge, where the altercation occurred, suggests he is a victim of racism since his establishment caters to an upscale black clientele. Atlanta Mayor Bill Campbell, a familiar fixture on the six o'clock news when posturing over the closing of Atlanta's notorious Gold Club, has been strangely low-key about Buckhead's problems. The Atlanta City Council, which has funded several hundred vacant police positions that haven't been filled, is all over the map as usual. The business leadership? Deafeningly silent. And that is the crux of the problem for Buckhead and the rest of Atlanta.

A familiar criticism of Atlanta is that if it could "suck like it can blow, it would have the Atlantic Ocean at its doorstep," meaning we aren't at all hesitant to pat ourselves on the back. For example, when it was announced that Super Bowl XXX-whatever was gracing the city with its presence, city poobahs were all over the media extolling the economic benefits and confirming the city's big league status. The bandwagon couldn't accommodate them all. Their gushing was exceeded only by that of the local Atlanta media. But, as of this writing, I haven't heard a public expression of concern from business leaders or business organizations about the damage that the publicity from the shootings and the Atlanta police's handling of the case have done to the city nationwide. Neither have I heard them demand that something to be done to fix the problem—like close the bars earlier and fill the vacant police positions.

There is a reason for the reticence. Everything in Atlanta is tinged by racial considerations. Any criticism by the predominately white business establishment of the predominately black political establishment risks public accusations of racism and private threats of retaliation. As a result, business leaders in Atlanta have lost their will to provide the necessary leadership to make politicians do the right thing. It is not worth the heat.

A prominent Atlanta businessman and good friend challenged me some months back for saying this and asserted that the business establishment is active behind the scenes on a number of issues in the city. If so, that is good. But it is not good enough. The public needs to know that Atlanta's business leaders are holding the city's politicians accountable for how they manage the city.

If somebody doesn't find a voice soon, Buckhead could go the way of downtown Atlanta in general and Underground Atlanta specifically. Look at a map. Atlanta has no boundaries and can grow in any direction. That means people who are able to can run away from their problems into neighboring counties. Many have, considering the staggering traffic problems of the metropolitan area. Those too poor to move become a tax burden on those who are left, including the business community.

The Buckhead murders can't be swept under the rug or buried behind some slick rah-rah marketing program. It is time for leadership. It is time for the CEOs of Atlanta's major corporations to step up and assert that leadership.

If they don't, who will?

The Dark Side
of Sunshine

February 21, 2000

Despite enactment of Governor Roy Barnes' much-heralded open-records law last year, the state's media still find too many local governments continuing to stonewall legitimate open-records requests. Meanwhile, telemarketing firms, agribusiness, trial attorneys and disgruntled state employees are using the law to create prospect lists, circumvent the legal discovery process, or just plain snoop on colleagues.

A survey by the Georgia First Amendment Foundation last fall found that less than half the city police, county sheriffs, and school superintendents complied with requests for public records, supposedly available to all citizens, when contacted by the media. Some reporters were threatened for even asking.

Contrast that with the University System of Georgia, which is besieged by open-records requests ranging from the sublime to the ridiculous. And nowhere is that more obvious than at the flagship institution, the University of Georgia. The UGA communications department employees two full-time employees—a manager and a secretary—just to coordinate the requests that pour in for information. Last fiscal year, that office handled some 140 requests. This fiscal year, with five months to go, requests are at 138 and climbing. Predominant on the list are zealous marketers who see a ready-made prospect list for the asking, and trial attorneys who want the university officials to manage their discovery process for them. Granted, the institutions can recover charges for copying materials and the hourly rate of its lowest-paid employees, but for the marketing firms and law firms, it's simply cheaper than if they were forced to do it themselves.

To catalog some of the nonmedia requests, I filed my own open-records request (make that 139!) and here are some of the things I found:

• The University of Florida wants to negotiate a new contract for its athletic director, so to find out how much the competition is paying, its attorneys filed an open-records request to see all the contracts on file for University of Georgia Athletic Director Vince Dooley.

• United Telesis, an out-of-state telemarketing firm, requests—and receives—the names of all UGA freshmen living in campus dormitories. Students are prime targets for all kinds of sales pitches. They are offered credit cards, long distance services, magazines and myriad other "opportunities." The institution can do nothing about it.

In fact, those seeking information are under no obligation to reveal why they are asking. Currently, students can sign a form saying they don't wish to be contacted, but the state attorney general's office can't stop marketers from requesting and receiving names under "directory information," which is included in open records.

• The College of Agriculture averages three to four open-records requests a week. Schaeffer's Specialized Lubricants files a request for a list of farmers in Grady, Decatur and Thomas counties. Purvis Pecans wants the same information for Berrien County pecan producers. Coastal Grain Company asks for a list of all cattle producers in the state. Hey, why spend the time putting a prospect list together when the law requires the University of Georgia to do it for you?

• An employee suspects that a colleague received a higher raise than he or she did. To confirm that suspicion—you guessed it—an open-records request allows an employee to peruse the previous evaluations and salary history of anybody within his or her department. In fact, employees can get most anything they want, short of medical records and patent information.

• Savell & Williams, an Atlanta law firm representing the State of Georgia in a suit-countersuit in the UGA art department, files a nine-page, 84-question letter of extraordinary detail, in effect having the UGA law department act as clerks while the firm is billing the state. (Note: While this firm is no longer representing the defendant, these kinds of requests from law firms are becoming the norm.) The plaintiff's attorney, Hue Henry, of course, has filed an open-records request to see what open-records requests have been filed by the other side!

And speaking of attorneys, Lee Parks, who is leading the effort to overturn the University of Georgia's admission policy, is a regular in filing open-records requests. To date, my examination of his requests shows that he has filed 11 times going back to July 1999. My examination also shows that Parks owes the University—and the taxpayers—$1,144.44. I can find no record that he has paid.

So while news organizations still have to pry the public's information from recalcitrant government bureaucracies, direct marketers, trial attorneys, and others seem to have a new low-cost secretarial service available to them. It is called the University of Georgia.

I wonder if this is what the governor had in mind when he advocated more openness in government?

Caring Parents
Key to
Better Schools

February 28, 2000

My son-in-law is a good teacher. How good? Last year, an Atlanta media conglomerate not known for being generous with its money gave him $10,000 and named him Teacher of the Year.

I was curious about how much interest he had in the education reform hullabaloo going on at the Capitol. The answer is, not much. It is not that he isn't interested in better education, but the fight looks very political to him—the governor versus the teachers unions. For example, the issue of tenure, which has the unions in a dither, is a nonissue to him. He doesn't need it. He is an outstanding teacher. He would like to get rid of bad teachers as much as the governor. On many occasions he has told me that education should be like business. Do well and be rewarded. Do poorly and lose your job.

He appreciates more direction in what to teach. He likes the idea of smaller classes and he certainly wants to be compensated fairly for his efforts. (I want that for him, too, for he is raising my grandsons.) But what he really wants, he isn't going to get out of the shouting and posturing and threatening among the proponents and opponents of education reform. Somebody needs to lower the decibel level and listen to him.

He wants parental involvement. Not the meddling kind of involvement from uninformed parents but real interest in what schools are doing. He wants parents to make their child's education a priority at home. He wants parents to support teachers and have confidence in their efforts to give Georgia's children a quality education. He believes, and I agree, that public education gets a bad rap and good teachers don't get the respect they deserve.

He says the top students in his high school are as good as the best students in private schools. He just doesn't have as many. The one thing that distinguishes his best students, he says, are parents who care about what kind of education their children are getting. These parents are familiar with the teachers and what they teach.

They check homework. They come to teacher conferences and ask good questions about the quality of the education their children are getting. But, most importantly, they let the teachers do their job.

Smaller class size, abolishing tenure, teacher accountability and all the other promises of education reform are just going to be so much window dressing if we don't find some way to make parents as accountable for motivating their children as we are making teachers responsible for teaching them. There are other deep-rooted problems in public education as well. *When the yelling stops at the Capitol maybe all parties will recognize their job has just begun.*

John Clendenin, the retired chairman of BellSouth Corporation, was rightfully known as the nation's "Education CEO." He was an articulate spokesman for public education, but politicians didn't like his message. They simply wanted to know how much money to allot to education. Mr. Clendenin's answer was that money alone wasn't the issue. It was all the other things that get in the way of educating a child—working parents, single parents, unmotivated parents, drugs, crime, poverty, violence.

Some of that mind-set is at work in the current education reform bill making its way through the Legislature. Much of the legislation is good. Most of it is well-meaning. But until we deal with the other issues impacting public education, this bill will have only a moderate impact on improving public education in Georgia.

A big point has been made about how business is supporting public education reform. Once this legislation is enacted into law, will business and the political establishment deal with the other issues that force us to put law enforcement officers, metal detectors and drug-sniffing dogs in our public schools? Or, will they assume their job is done and that weapon searches are going to be as common as the three Rs?

Not only will my son-in-law be impacted by what happens, but so will my son, who is in the process of earning his teaching certificate. To say I have a vested interest in the answer is an understatement.

The Delta
We Knew and Loved
Is Gone Forever

While the Transport Workers Union failed to unionize the 11,000 baggage and cargo handlers at Delta Air Lines, the vote made an important point: The Delta we once loved and now love to hate, will never the be the same again.

Perhaps this is practicing psychology without a license but in the South we long have felt like underdogs to our more sophisticated brethren up north. We looked for examples of our own home-made superiority. Obviously, Example One was Coca-Cola, first bottled in Joseph Pemberton's drug store in Atlanta. Then, there was good ol' Delta Air Lines, begun as a crop dusting service in Monroe, Louisiana. The thing we liked about Delta is

It reflected what we believe to be our uniqueness—Southern hospitality.

Delta's friendly personnel and the foresight of its early CEOs—like founder C.E. Woolman, Charlie Dolson, Tom Beebe, and Dave Garrett—helped propel the regional airline into a national competitor. The smiling, courteous service made us feel special, particularly if you compared it to the rude, scowling Eastern Air Lines personnel. Word got around that Delta was something special. And it was.

In the very early '60s, Delta made the first of three strategic decision that changed things forever for the carrier. While Eastern and others were busy adding propjets to their fleet, Delta leap-frogged that phase and went straight to jets. It was, in my opinion, a turning point for the airline. Now the gracious, personal service was combined with speed and ease of travel. Delta was off and running.

In the late '70s as Delta was gearing up to go international, airline deregulation landed on the industry with a splat. Airline travel went from something special to the equivalent of riding an aerial Greyhound bus, and a seesaw effect took place: Fares went down, passenger miles went up, service went down, complaints went up.

It was in this new environment that Delta made its second critical decision. The carrier decided to compete head-to-head with the big boys at United, American, TWA and Pan Am. There was no other choice really, because it was "eat or be eaten." Delta first acquired Western Air Lines. Then, they made the big step by acquiring the European routes of Pan Am, the venerable and sophisticated airline but a financial loser. With these moves, Delta's uniqueness was gone. Too many people were now in the company who didn't appreciate, understand or, frankly, care about Delta's old culture.

The customers were the first to notice. Most of us locals felt we had a special contract with Delta and that they had broken that contract. We still wanted the same pleasant, smiling service of the '60s but the cheap fares of the '90s. However, Delta was in the big leagues now. The Southern charm was jettisoned. To survive in that league you've got to watch the bottom line closely. That is when the third critical decision was made. Ron Allen, the CEO at the time, took an ax to the firm, cutting staff and wages, outsourcing work formerly done by Delta employees, perhaps saving the company from financial ruin but destroying morale in the process.

Now, Leo Mullin, Delta's first CEO from outside the family, has inherited an unsettled environment—dispirited employees and disappointed customers. He has also inherited a major player in the aviation industry. His Delta Air Lines last year carried 110 million, 20 percent more than its nearest competitor. The little crop duster is a heavyweight today.

The TWU's failure indicates a short grace period by most of the 72,000 employees who want to see if Mullin can restore morale and revive the "Delta family." But he has his work cut out for him. The old Delta is gone, because the days when flying was something special are gone also.

The world has changed and, unfortunately, Delta has had to change with it.

Don't Tinker with Lottery or HOPE

In all of the rhetoric swirling around the state Capitol on education reform, I find it ironic almost no mention has been made about the HOPE Scholarship Program and the Georgia Lottery. In my opinion, the debate about education reform stems from those state initiatives. HOPE has had an enormously positive impact on the quality of higher education in Georgia, and now we have to fix the "feeder system"—the public schools.

The omission of the lottery and HOPE from the political debates is even more ironic because our state government has conducted these programs extremely well. One can only hope that our political leaders are as successful with education reform as with the lottery.

Let's give credit where credit is due. Former Governor Zell Miller was a political genius to propose the lottery, get it passed against stiff opposition from powerful church groups, designate proceeds for educational purposes and then ensure that the monies raised from the lottery wouldn't be deducted from the education budget as the legislature in Florida has done. The lottery-education connection is a home run.

Then he, or somebody, had the extremely good fortune to convince Rebecca Paul to serve as president of the Georgia Lottery Corporation. Another home run. Under Paul's leadership, the Georgia Lottery has hummed like a well-oiled machine. Every year since its inception in 1993, the Georgia Lottery Corporation has increased sales—the only U.S. lottery to do so—surpassing $2 billion for the past fiscal year and paying out over $1 billion to players during the same term.

Most important, the lottery has transferred almost $3.2 billion to the State of Georgia's educational programs. Remember, our education system would not otherwise have that $3.2 billion.

While the lottery has funded Georgia's pre-kindergarten program and over $1.35 billion in capital outlays for computers and other technological upgrades for schools and colleges throughout the state, the extraordinary HOPE Scholarship Program has had the most impact.

As I travel around the country, I find people disbelieving that any student who graduates from a Georgia high school with at least a B average can attend college in our state and have their tuition and mandatory fees paid and get a book allowance to boot. By the end of 1999, almost a half-million young Georgians have earned HOPE scholarships since the program began six years ago. The result has been a dramatic increase in the quality of students attending the state's colleges and universities.

Look no further than my alma mater, the University of Georgia. The Scholastic Assessment Test (SAT) scores for the 1999 freshmen average 1200, and they continue to rise with each freshman class. Not bad for a university with no engineering school and no medical school. Today, our top high school seniors who once sought admission to out-of-state universities and had UGA as their backup choice, are clamoring to get in. Some families have resorted to hiring lawyers to overturn the University's admissions policy. Parents have told me that, given how much money they save as a result of HOPE, they will buy their kid a new car and still save money.

Incredibly, some people still disapprove of the lottery, despite its enormous contributions it has made to education. Their reasoning escapes me. Some Bible thumpers call lotteries "godless," but then so is the Super Bowl. Some say that the lottery targets poor people who can least afford the money to play, but I haven't been furnished any statistics that say people are any poorer because we have a lottery. Some folks oppose it because they are against gambling of any kind. I would assume that includes office pools and bingo.

As for myself, I have two concerns about the Georgia Lottery. How long can we keep Rebecca Paul, and how long before somebody in the governor's office or the General Assembly decides to tinker with the program and muck up one of our state's greatest success stories? To the former concern, I would suggest doing whatever it takes to keep Ms. Paul happy. Her record speaks for itself.

And if anybody in state government is contemplating messing with the lottery, call me first. I can think of at least a few hundred other things in our state that need your attention more.

If I'm not in, ask for Zell Miller.

Can't Whup Up
on Fightin' Murphs
Anymore

Is it just me or was this the most do-nothing legislative session in recent memory? Maybe "do-nothing" is too strong a term. In fairness, our state legislators did do something. They did whatever Governor Roy Barnes told them to. The governor rolled them like a cheap cigar.

Maybe members of the General Assembly just naturally share political philosophy with the governor or maybe they want to be sure that they didn't get their name on Barnes' Naughty List, a compilation of who voted as they were told to and who didn't. Evidently, if you didn't vote with the governor at least 90 percent of the time, you don't get invited to the Mansion Christmas party and can't get a one-lane cow path paved in your district.

There was one notable show of legislative independence during the past session, however. With no wink or nod from Governor Barnes signaling them what to do, our intrepid solons decided to tackle a major education reform issue on their own. As a result of their swift action, competition has been outlawed in Haralson County. I am talking, of course, about the Bremen High School Protection Act of 2000. In case you missed this brouhaha, House Speaker Tom Murphy, who just happens to represent that area, has gotten frustrated because his beloved Bremen High School can't even beat a drum. It seems that just about everybody, but mainly those uppity private schools in Atlanta, have been whuppin' up on their ball teams and especially their debate team. Oh, did I mention that the Speaker's daughter-in-law is the coach of the Bremen High debate team?

Murphy decided damned if he was going to sit in the stands on chilly October nights and see the Fighting Murphs constantly knocked on their cans and then go into some steamy classroom and see the same thing happen to Haralson County's future silver-tongued orators.

So, an aggrieved Speaker presented his plight to a stunned and indignant Legislature eager to make things right for ol' Bremen

High. Their answer was to jump all private schools up two levels in the Georgia High School Association's classification system this year. This means that Bremen High School's toughest opponent next year likely will be Mother's Morning Out Day Care Center. To the remaining high schools in our state—public and private—there has begun a domino effect of rescheduling games in time for next fall's football season. But that is nowhere near as important as keeping the Speaker happy. Let's face it, if there is anything Bremen is known for besides making cheap suits and losing debates and ballgames, it is the fact that it is Tom Murphy territory and don't you forget it.

Now that the 2000 session is history, there are two schools of thought on the current state of our Legislature. One is that it is not representative of the people who elected them but, rather, is a conduit for rubber-stamping the governor's programs. Others say that is not all bad because we are not subjected to the kind of perpetual gridlock we see in Washington, where even selecting a chaplain gets to be partisan, let alone trying to pass legislation. At least if you don't like what is going on in Georgia, you have only one place to look—the governor's office.

Thankfully, we have had a long string of good governors—honest, progressive and innovative. Even though the Legislature has more females, minorities and Republicans than ever before, it hasn't kept pace. If anything, it has gotten more docile, acting more like a part of the executive branch of government than an independent Legislative branch. Still, there are some rewards for doing as you are told. At least legislators still get to dip into the pork barrel before they go home to explain how hard they fought for their constituents in Atlanta.

One last note on the Georgia General Assembly. One of its most imposing members is calling it quits, and the Legislature will be poorer for it. Senator Mike Egan (R-Atlanta), who has been a committed and, yes, fiercely independent public servant for the past three decades, has announced his retirement. In this session, he spent much of his time helping to level the playing field for female athletes in Georgia who historically have been denied the same opportunities as their male counterparts. It is called gender equity.

No word on whether or not it will be permitted in Bremen.

The Braves' New
Touchy-Feely Game

In case you have been too caught up in the saga of the federal government's conspiracy against beloved-terrorist-turned-imam H. Rap Brown, you probably haven't noticed that another baseball season is upon us. It is time to once again get our hopes up with the Atlanta Braves, who have turned "near-miss" into an art form over the past decade.

But this year, sports fans, things are going to be different. The Braves are serious about bringing a World Series championship back home. They have hired a sensitivity coach.

Play (politically correct) Ball!

Just think. When the Bravos are waxed by the Yankees, Mets, Reds or whoever next September, as they no doubt will be, our heroes can gather in center field, hold hands, and sing, "Kum Ba Yah." Don't you just love it? No longer will a 97-mile-an-hour fastball be enough. Now, the players must be touchy-feely, too.

Somehow, I have the sneaking suspicion that this development is a direct result of the embarrassment caused by the blathering of the team's ace reliever and designated motor mouth, John Rocker, to a *Sports Illustrated* reporter a few of months ago. Never mind First Amendment issues, Rocker has put the Braves squarely in the gun sights of special interest groups like the Concerned Black Clergy, who need his hide in order to get much-needed television face time.

Explaining the need for sensitivity training, Stan Kasten, president of the Braves, "We take the business of our community relations and our image in the community very seriously." Bull. If that was the case, the organization would discourage the Tomahawk Chop, which Native Americans find offensive. This isn't about being good citizens. It is about trying to mollify a group of demagogues. Just as the Braves can't win the big one, they can't take the heat from a few mean-spirited preachers who couldn't find the word *forgiveness* in the Bible if you spotted them the first five books.

If they were serious about sensitivity training, they would have had their leader, Ted Turner, sitting on the front row. What Rocker said in one interview, Atlanta's own looney tune has managed to say over a number of years. Turner has insulted Christians ("Christianity is for losers."), Jews ("I know what it is like to be rounded up and sent to the East somewhere and resettled."), Italians ("They'd rather be involved in crime and making some wine and just have a good time."), Haitians ("Haitians breed like cats."), and the Pope (When asked what he would say if he met the Holy Father, Turner said he would hold up his foot and say, "Ever seen a Polish mine detector?")

Rocker gets the special-interest crowd hyperventilating because he is an easy target. Like shooting fish in a barrel. Turner? It seems he is a different situation. Were the Concerned Black Clergy upset by his depiction of Christianity as a religion for "losers"? Not a peep. Did the Baseball Commissioner threaten to suspend him for his slurs against various ethnic groups? Not a chance. Did Stan Kasten invite him to sensitivity training along with the jocks? I doubt it very seriously.

What we are dealing with is a double standard. When you have a few billion dollars to sling around, as does Mr. Turner, people tend to overlook a few slurs here and there. It is hard to be angry while holding your hand out.

If the Braves had only asked, I could have saved them the grief in which they now find themselves and a few bucks on sensitivity training. Any organization that would allow a puffed-up and self-important kid like John Rocker to strut and preen with a reporter from a national magazine unsupervised, needs more than the words to "We Are the World." It needs a new public relations staff.

No public relations person I know would have let the Rocker interview occur without some coaching beforehand. An organization as concerned about their image as the Braves claim to be would have had a public relations representative there during the entire interview. They asked for trouble and they got it.

But, all is well that ends well. The Braves are now sensitive. The Concerned Black Clergy has cowed another victim. Prices are still too high at the ballpark. Turner is still rich and still acting like a clown. Native Americans are still offended by the Tomahawk Chop. It's baseball time again.

Kum Ba Yah!

Gowen's Integrity
and Class
Always in Style

Permit me a point of personal privilege. Unless you are my age or a student of Georgia politics, you might not know the name Charles Gowen.

From 1939 until 1960, Gowen was a major force on the state political scene as a member of the Georgia House of Representatives from Glynn County. Through his influence the state bought Jekyll Island in the late '40s. In 1954, he lost the governor's race to Marvin Griffin and soon after retired from politics to devote himself to a long and distinguished career as an attorney with the Atlanta law firm of King & Spalding.

I was honored to have the opportunity to present Gowen with a special award at the University of Georgia annual alumni luncheon, which this year celebrated the 75th anniversary of his graduation. To give that some perspective, when Gowen left Athens with his law degree in hand, the University of Georgia had less than two thousand students (it now has 34,000). The entire state's population (2.8 million) was less than metropolitan Atlanta's today. Republican Calvin Coolidge was in his second year as president, and former attorney general Clifford Mitchell Walker was Georgia's governor.

My first exposure to Charlie Gowen came in 1990 in, of all places, Biarritz, France. We were on a University of Georgia tour and bravely I walked up and introduced myself. "Mr. Gowen," I said, "my name is Dick Yarbrough and I want you to know that when I became eligible to vote, I voted for you in the governor's race." If I was expecting a "Gee, thanks," I had badly miscalculated. Instead, he said, "Young man, if everybody who told me that had done that, I would have been governor." Straight-to-the-point, as I was to learn, is a Charlie Gowen trademark.

While he can sometimes be coaxed into reminiscing about his days in the General Assembly, Gowen tends, at 96, to look forward and not back. He still drives his car, still enjoys an evening out, and still maintains a passion for the University of Georgia.

I have asked him several times about writing a book but he's not interested. His stories would make a great read. Consider one of his first court cases. Fresh out of law school, he was asked to defend a black man on St. Simons Island who had a nightclub, Sam's Emporium, that was being encroached on by a new white development. So many spectators showed up for the trial that it had to be moved from the one-room courthouse to the pier overlooking the ocean. As the trial progressed and Charlie began his closing arguments, several jurors left their seats and jumped into the ocean. They went to the rescue of a summer resident crying for help. After the swimmer was safely on shore, Gowen finished his closing arguments and the soggy jurors found in his favor. Sam's Emporium was saved.

Then there was the night in 1946 when Georgia could claim three governors. Eugene Talmadge, who had just won election, had died before he could be sworn in. His son, Herman, was elected by the legislature to succeed him, but the State Constitution supported the succession of the lieutenant governor, M.E. Thompson. The outgoing governor, Ellis Arnall, refused to give up the office to young Talmadge. Word was received that a group of Talmadge supporters were coming to break down the doors and take over. Rumors were that someone had a gun. A number of legislators, including Gowen, were guarding the door to the governor's office, just in case that happened. It was a tense moment. As he waited for the mob to approach, Gowen asked one of his fellow legislators, "Where is security?" He wasn't pleased to hear that the governor's security officer had climbed out the window and was headed for parts unknown!

That story and others like it make an interesting point. Politics were a lot more interesting in those days and maybe even more fun, but not necessarily better. Rural Georgia dominated through the county-unit system. Blacks were excluded from the mainstream and that misnomer, "Separate but equal," was the law.

Today, our Legislature is more urban, has an impressive contingent of minorities and women, and is more sophisticated and progressive by light-years than "the good old days." But one thing that deliberative body could always use more of is a few good Charlie Gowens.

His brand of integrity and class never go out of style.

Reminds Me of the Black Telephone Days

May 8, 2000

I have seen the future and I don't like what I see.

It is called mega-merger and resulted in the recent fight between a Mickey Mouse organization, called Walt Disney Company and the Looney Tunes bunch at AOL/Time Warner/Ted Turner, or whatever their name is this week.

Time Warner had a dispute with Disney over programming issues so they decided to even the score by pulling the plug on Disney's ABC subsidiary in those areas of the country served by their cable system. Fortunately, a temporary truce was crafted and for the time being, customers can watch ABC on Time Warner cable, but this is not going to be the last fight between those who provide programming and those who distribute it—and there is nothing you and I can do about it.

What happened between these two behemoths ought to be of great concern to you. I'm not just talking about missing "Who Wants to Be a Millionaire?" I am talking about information control. Your ability to get unfettered news from unbiased sources is rapidly disappearing with the current media mega-mergers. Disney owns ABC. Viacom owns CBS. General Electric owns NBC. Time Warner owns Turner, CNN, and *Time* magazine. These are multibillion-dollar conglomerates in control of networks, programming, movies, publishing. They control what you can see, hear and read. I also am not comforted by the fact that the *Chicago Tribune* just bought the *Los Angeles Times* and that the *New York Times* bought the *Boston Globe*. We are on the way to a national monopoly on information.

It is not just the media mergers that scare me. It is the whole trend toward bigness. When divestiture of the Bell System occurred in 1984, there were seven new companies created to compete in the telecommunications marketplace. Today, there are four, going on three. Bell Atlantic bought Nynex first and GTE next. Southwestern Bell, now SBC, swallowed up PacTel and Ameritech. Somebody named Global Crossing is absorbing US West. That leaves my alma mater, BellSouth, once the largest of the Baby Bells and now a middleweight, except for its wireless operations, which have just been merged with SBCs.

The same thing is happening in the banking, insurance and automobile industries as well. All the companies say they have to get bigger in order to compete in the international marketplace.

Know what happens when everybody gets bigger? You and I get smaller as a priority. Anybody who thinks we are going to be better served by mega-mergers is either naïve or is writing the conglomerate's press releases. When was the last time you called a large company and got a human being on the other end? When was the last time you got called back to see if your complaint had been handled to your satisfaction? You and I are expensive to companies, and wasting assets like people on us is not a good use of their resources. As a matter of fact, people are a tremendous cost to business and the less of them you have, the better. If we need to talk to someone, we can just punch a bunch of numbers on the telephone. That's a lot better on the bottom line.

I called an Atlanta-based organization last week and after banging numbers to get where I thought I wanted to go and not getting there, I pushed "0" for the operator. I waited through 27 rings. On the 28th, I was answered and instructed to hold. I held for seven seconds short of four minutes. Then I was transferred to my requested department and got another recording! I've got to think that this outfit feels pretty good about the money it is saving in personnel costs. Hopefully, they never have to call themselves on the telephone.

Companies wax eloquent that bigness means more customer choice. I don't agree. It means more choice from fewer sources. It reminds me of an old line from Bell System monopoly days. You can have any choice of telephone color you want—just as long as it is black. Looks like those days are coming back.

Two days before the Disney Time-Warner fight, Steve Case, CEO of AOL, which has bought Time-Warner, said, "Business development and social responsibility must go hand-in-hand. Look beyond making money in order to build a medium we can be proud of." Then his cable company pulled the plug on its customers.

In the early 1900s, robber baron Cornelius Vanderbilt said, "The public be damned." At least he was honest about it.

Make Parents
Responsible
for Kids
June 5, 2000

The last thing we need in this state is more laws, but I've got an idea for one I think might be worth the time and attention of our legislators. They aren't going to have much to do next year other than deal with a small matter of whether or not to change the state flag. That shouldn't take long. They have already gotten the big issue out of the way with the Bremen High School Protection Act that makes it illegal to beat the Fightin' Murphs at anything.

My idea is to hold parents totally responsible for their kids. Novel idea, isn't it?

If a kid brings a gun to school, go arrest the parents and throw their fannies in jail. If their child sasses a teacher or cuts class or sneaks out behind the school to smoke pot, go find either parent, or both, and have them write, "I have done a sorry job of raising my child and I apologize" on the blackboard a few hundred times.

If Junior or Sis doesn't turn in their homework, give the parents one day to do it on their child's behalf, grade the work and if it isn't A material, make them do it over until it is.

If their male child shows up with his underwear showing over his pants and his hair down to his waist, make Momma and Daddy write a 5000-word essay on good grooming. Again, if it isn't A material, do it over.

Recently at St. Simons, I was awakened at 5:30 A.M. by a bunch of teenagers cavorting in a hot tub at the condominium where we were staying. If the law I am proposing is passed, we will be able to go into their homes, wake their no-good parents, and have them stand at attention in the hot sun for the next 24 hours. That would take care of any future problems.

While we are at it, let's talk about having young people saying "yes ma'am" and "no sir." That seems to be on the minds of a lot of people these days. Of course, we want that chore placed on the schools, not in the home. Let me give you a clue. I said, "ma'am" and "sir" without the school's help and at my advanced age, I still do. My daddy told me to. He had this simple notion that he set the rules of my conduct, not the education system. Therefore, my law would require that any child who can't be polite when addressing an adult watch Mama and Daddy get their mouths washed out with soap. What happens then would be between the parents and the child when they got home. The law wouldn't be specific about that.

I think my law also would effectively deal with the issue of the separation of church and state. Many people want to see prayer in the school, feeling, I assume, that the public school system should also be responsible for their children's religious training as well. That is going to be impossible under the education reforms mandated by Governor Barnes. Right now, schools can't find enough time for PE or band practice, let alone trying to squeeze in prayer. So here is what my law would do. Anybody who feels strongly about prayer in the schools would have to turn in a signed affidavit to the local board of education that they had attended a church, synagogue or mosque for 52 straight weeks as a family and had been seen on their knees, praying to God for wisdom and guidance on how to become a better parent, husband, wife, son, daughter, etc. With that, their kids could go out behind the school where they used to smoke pot and pray instead. (Governor, if you are interested, I would be willing to amend my proposal to pray also for more time for band practice and physical education.)

There may be an item or two I have missed, but we have time to refine the proposed legislation. School is out. Teachers have a few months to rest up before they once again begin their babysitting service for parents who don't have time to raise their kids. We can take down the metal detectors, wave good-bye to the school police, wash and groom the drug-sniffing dogs. In August, we can start the whole thing over.

By then, I will have my legislation ready for the General Assembly. Can there be anybody in opposition?

Dear Roy: Don't Pander to the Press

June 12, 2000

Honorable Roy Barnes
State Capitol

Dear Governor:

As you know, I am one of your biggest fans. I think you have done an outstanding job as governor and I have said so in my columns and in speeches around the state. But today I am not a happy camper.

You are being lobbied shamelessly by Colin Campbell, a columnist for the *Atlanta Journal-Constitution* to foist more than 5000 boxes of Olympic junk off on the University System of Georgia—and the taxpayers. I think it's time you heard the other side of the story. First, most of the boxes in question were located in the State of Georgia archives until September 1997 when the Olympic folks were told to come take them off the state's hands. They did and began an effort of deciding which boxes were worth saving and which weren't. It takes an average of six hours to read through a box just to know. The price for this thoroughness was accusations that brought the reputations and the integrity of these people into question and that is a shame. They deserve better. Campbell knows better.

The archiving process done by Atlanta History Center professionals produced some 900 boxes that have material considered to be of historic value. Since July 19, 1999—almost a year ago—those 900 boxes and, in fact all 6000 boxes, have been available for Colin Campbell or anyone else to view. To my knowledge, he has made less than five trips to the Atlanta History Center to look at them. Now, he is lobbying Chancellor Steve Portch and you to accept the 5000 or so remaining boxes of junk. I can't for the life of me understand why. If he can't get to the Atlanta History Center from downtown Atlanta, why would he drive 20 miles to Kennesaw State or 75 miles to UGA or 100 miles to Macon State?

The boxes at the Atlanta History Center are being paid for privately, not by the taxpayers, just like the Games themselves. If you force the University of Georgia or any other institution in the state to take the boxes that are deemed not of historical value, here is an example of what you are sticking the taxpayers with: Boxes of blank forms for people wanting to volunteer for the Games, several boxes of advertising slicks—or pictures—of the woebegone Olympic mascot, Izzy, and 30 to 40 boxes of forms used in the venues when someone needed first aid. Really historic stuff.

As you and I both know, the university system has grown in stature and reputation. We are the envy of other states. One reason is that the system has had the strong support of you and your predecessors. For another, it hasn't had overt political pressure put on it since the days of Gene Talmadge. I spend a lot more time in Athens than Colin Campbell, and I can tell you that if the University of Georgia wanted those boxes of junk, they would have asked for them. They don't want them. They don't have room for them. They don't need them. And the boxes should not be forced on them or any other institution to pacify one columnist.

I don't like seeing the University of Georgia and the other units of the university system placed in the position of pawns to satisfy one writer, and I am tired of my friends at the Atlanta Committee for the Olympic Games being cast as heavies. Neither can fight back, but I can.

If you or Chancellor Portch decides to accommodate him, how will you explain to taxpayers that what they are paying for isn't worth a cup of warm spit? Olympic scholars aren't standing in line to see who skinned a knee during the Centennial Olympic Games. Everybody seems to understand this but Colin Campbell.

Governor, there is nobody on the horizon that stands a snowball's chance in you-know-where of beating you in 2002. You know it and I know it. Your record is solid as a rock. You are headed toward being one of our best governors ever and you can do it without having to worry about one nagging columnist. Therefore, I have the solution for you.

Tell Campbell that if he wants those boxes so badly to come pick them up and store them at his house. Then you can get on with the serious business of the state.

I'll even find Izzy and help him with the move.

Your friend,

Dick Yarbrough

Of Baptists
and Women
Pastors

In case you missed it, the Southern Baptists are holding their annual confab this month in Orlando—home of the godless Walt Disney World—to affirm that women aren't fit to be ministers. It seems that through some kind of loophole, a hundred or so women got to be Baptist preachers, and while I have been unable to uncover any evidence that any or all of them did a poor job, nonetheless they are toast.

The statement of belief to be adopted at the convention reads: "While both men and women are gifted for service in the church, the office of pastor is limited to men as qualified by Scripture." So there!

But all is not lost. Women are directed by the Southern Baptist Convention "to forsake resistance to the authority of their respective husbands and to practice willing, joyful submission to that leadership." This is where I begin to get concerned. While I am Methodist, I fear that somebody in the leadership of my denomination will take a brief respite from trying to ordain gays and making all our hymns gender-neutral and adopt a measure similar to the Baptists. If that happens, I am sunk. After 42 years of marriage, to face the prospects of leadership in my household is a scary thing. Does this mean that my wife in practicing "willing, joyful submission" to my leadership is going to make me balance the checkbook? In order to do that, will I first have to learn how to write a check? Will I have to make my own doctor's appointments and then remember to show up when I am supposed to? Will I have to deal with the exterminator and the trash collector and contractors who say they are going to come on a certain day to work on the house but never do?

I am also concerned for my son and my son-in-law. I'd like to be there when they explain to their spouses that they are taking over and expecting said daughter and daughter-in-law to show a little " joyful submission." If they are contemplating such foolishness, I would suggest they first remove all the frying pans in the house because there is no question that both are going to get a skillet across the skull.

In the meantime, I am frantically scouring the Bible looking for some authority to give back the leadership to my wife. I don't want it.

Speaking of the Bible, the Southern Baptists offer no apologies for their hard-line approach and say that their Report on the Baptist Faith and Message is "thoroughly biblical. Every line is deeply rooted in the clear teaching of Scripture." If that is the case, then they have another loophole bigger than a bread box they need to close. It seems that the Reverend Charles Stanley, senior minister of the 13,000-member First Baptist Church of Atlanta, recently got divorced. According to the SBC, "Marriage is a covenant commitment to the exclusive, permanent, monogamous union of one man and one woman, and thus it cannot be defined as a flexible contract between consenting human beings." I think that says that divorce is a no-no and that this would apply to Rev. Stanley.

However, I haven't heard as much clamor that Stanley, a former president of the Southern Baptist Convention, should resign his post as I have about getting rid of women preachers. Although I am confused over what looks to be a blatant double standard, I am certain that I will hear from those who will enlighten me on the subject. It won't be the first time.

During my tenure at the Atlanta Committee for the Olympic Games, I heard quite often from those who opposed something we were doing in the most intemperate, harsh, mean-spirited language possible. For a religion that is supposed to be built on Love Thy Neighbor, I could only assume that meant that the neighbor had to think like we think, act like we act and believe as we believe.

All of the furor reminds me of the story of the angel giving the tour of heaven. As they would pass a cloud full of other angels, she would announce what denomination was represented. Finally approaching one cloud of dour-looking angels, a tourist asked, "Who is that?" "Shh," admonished the angel, "Don't let them see you. They think they are the only ones here!"

Now, if you will excuse me, I am going to exert some leadership—assuming it's okay with my wife.

"Crash" Oxendine
Proves a Point

A little public affairs pop quiz, readers. What are the duties of the Georgia secretary of state? The labor commissioner? What about the insurance commissioner? Who is the commissioner of agriculture? Who heads up the corrections department? The revenue department?

Chances are that most of us don't have a clue who these people are or what they do. Yet, some—attorney general, agriculture, education, labor, insurance—are elected by us. Others—corrections, transportation, natural resources, industry and trade, revenue, public safety—are appointed. Why do we elect some and appoint others? Does that mean some jobs are more important than others? Are we any better off with an elected attorney general and secretary of state? Should we also elect the revenue commissioner and the transportation commissioner?

Why don't we also elect the cabinet members in Washington? What is the difference in electing a state commissioner of agriculture and having the president appoint a secretary of agriculture in Washington?

Some of the department head jobs in Georgia seem to be parking places for those contemplating a run for governor. That is rumored to be the case with our secretary of state (Cathy Cox, in case you didn't know), who is being whispered as successor to Governor Roy Barnes in 2006. Mike Bowers, former attorney general, all but wore a "I am running for governor" sign around his neck until he forgot to tell a fawning capitol press corps about his extracurricular activities.

And then there is John Oxendine. He is your insurance commissioner, your fire safety commissioner, your industrial loan commissioner and somehow still finds time to be your comptroller general. We elected him in 1994 and reelected him in 1998.

Oxendine is a name that comes up often as a Republican candidate for—surprise!—governor. While it is not spelled out in Commissioner Oxendine's long list of job responsibilities, he also gets a blue light for his state-owned vehicle. Big mistake. A recent news report revealed that last fall, he totaled his state-owned vehicle (meaning that it is owned by you and me) to the tune of $19,000 responding to what he said was a "hazardous materials call" at the state government complex. This is the second car you and I have bought him. He did more than $17,000 in damage to another one four years ago dodging a deer in Gwinnett County.

According to the police who investigated the most recent incident, Commissioner Oxendine was driving lickety-split toward downtown Atlanta and was forced to stop at a red light at South Atlanta Road in Cobb County. Deciding time was a-wastin', he whipped out his trusty blue light in order to run the red light and promptly collided with a pickup truck. Fortunately, neither driver was hurt. How about those poor bureaucrats at the state government offices for whom the commissioner risked life and limb? Seems like they didn't know they were in danger because as of this writing, no one can find a report of any alarm at any state government building that day. The Georgia Building Authority reports they even checked with Georgia State University and the MARTA station nearby for any reported alarms and came up empty.

Now both the state attorney general's office and the Georgia Bureau of Investigation are looking into how Oxendine could hear an alarm in Cobb County that nobody in downtown Atlanta could hear. Which brings up an interesting point. If Oxendine reported to the governor and didn't have a good answer about why he was flashing his blue lights like a Kmart special, he likely would not be the current insurance/fire safety/industrial loan/comptroller general. Roy Barnes would have already sent him packing. As for the voters, we've got to wait until 2002 to make Oxendine answerable for his Barney Fife imitation.

I don't know about you, but I don't feel any more qualified to judge the qualifications for the insurance commissioner or the agriculture commissioner than I do voting on Lawrence Summers to be U.S. Secretary of the Treasury. We need a constitutional amendment to let the governor appoint the state heads. That way we can be more assured that state government is pulling in the same direction and is not an amalgamation of individual fiefdoms, some appointed and some elected; some loyal, some not. I think you would see a much more efficient government answerable to the governor who, in turn, is answerable to us.

Just think of the money we would save on blue lights and wrecked automobiles.

An Idea
Worthy of
Looney Tunes

July 3, 2000

I noticed that Robb Pitts, president of the Atlanta City Council and a mayoral candidate, is proposing to sell naming rights to Hartsfield International Airport, much as the free-loading professional sports teams have done. Mr. Pitts says he was inspired by the fact that Philips Electronics is paying $20 million a year for 20 years to have its name on the arena in Atlanta that hosts the two biggest losers in town, the Hawks and the Thrashers. That kind of corporate reasoning makes me hesitant to plug in one of their toasters.

As I understand it, he wouldn't just sell the airport rights, he'd sell the individual concourses. Can't you just see it now? You park in the Burger King parking lot and enter the Bank of America terminal to get your ticket. From there, you are directed to the Men's Warehouse concourse. That is, of course, after you have been checked out at the Dunkin' Donuts security checkpoint.

If Pitts wants to pursue this idea through to its logical conclusion, I would suggest that he also encourage Delta Airlines to sell their coach section to a sardine packing company. It would be a natural.

He reasons that if the Ted Turner/Looney Tunes/AOL/Time-Warner mega-conglomerate can get such big bucks for showcasing ineptitude, think what Atlanta could get for its airport, which is about the only thing in the city that works. Mr. Pitts thinks his idea is worth the look because Atlanta is a "cutting edge" city.

I hate to burst his balloon, but this is not a new idea. Back when a group of us were trying to get the town ready for the Olympic Games, the city's marketing department came up with a "cutting edge" program to sell streets, parks, buildings, and just about anything else they could get their hands on to the highest bidder. There was even some talk of bouncing laser-beam ads off the moon until the city's crack legal department determined that, alas, Atlanta didn't own the moon. Not to be deterred, the city ended up selling its soul in the form of a street-vending program that looked like a flea market on steroids while the local news media and the business community dithered. That effort brought us worldwide scorn and netted the city a cool $2.5 million. At least we found out what Atlanta thinks its reputation is worth.

But let's not be too harsh on Mr. Pitts. There may be some merit in his idea. For example, the city remains 400 police short of having a full contingent and shows no signs of ever filling the void. Therefore, let's sell the police department. If the police ever stopped you—highly unlikely unless you are an NFL linebacker with an attitude—you might notice their shirts with the "Acme Well Drilling and Tree Stump Removal" logo. The city could take the proceeds from that corporate sale and hire the cops it was unable to hire with the $2.5 million it made off of trashing downtown.

I see no end to the opportunities. The state would be wise to get in on the action. We could probably get a fortune from our highway system alone. Just think how easy it will be to direct some poor soul from Quebec trying to get to Florida: "Just take the Home Depot I-75 and hang a right onto I-475, sponsored by your local Coca-Cola bottler. That is, unless, you choose to go down Winn-Dixie Way, formerly I-16." The state highway department could take those much-needed dollars and pave over what little green space we still have left.

Despite his enthusiasm for it, I don't think Mr. Pitts' airport scheme is going to fly. Or at least I hope not. Instead of spending his time on this cockamamie idea, he might want to focus on making the city work. Close the bars down at a decent hour, run off illegal street vendors and panhandlers, get the police force up to strength, pick up the trash, encourage the business community to come out of hiding and help put some quality of life back in the city, get away from the obsession on race and understand that what happens in Atlanta—good or bad—affects the rest of the state.

But all is not lost. I think there is an excellent chance that he could sell his idea to Disney. It is just Mickey Mouse enough that they might buy it.

For Once,
The Good Guys Won

July 10, 2000

The Supreme Court of the United States just concluded its most recent term with a number of landmark decisions. Among the more noteworthy actions, the justices reaffirmed the so-called Miranda Law that requires criminal suspects be made aware of their rights before being questioned. Partial-birth abortion bans were struck down, as were group prayers at high school football games. No doubt, special interest groups were gleefully high-fiving each other over the rulings in the high court.

But the cheering stopped when the Court said that the Boy Scouts of America have the right to set their own standards for who can be a troop leader and who can't. This was a major setback for gay rights advocates who have been lobbying for years to force the Boy Scouts to accept them as Scout leaders. The Supreme Court by a regrettably small margin said "no" and in the process probably ruined a lot of bridespersons showers in Vermont, home of the same-sex marriage mill.

According to the Associated Press, critics predict the tent is going to fall in on the Boy Scouts because the organization has "squandered a reputation for tolerance" and will "face an erosion of public support." Those wonderfully unbiased folks at the American Civil Liberties Union opined that "People are going to turn to their local governments and say 'This is a pack of bigots. Don't give them special treatment.'" And the ACLU isn't bigoted? I can't think of a group on earth that is in less touch with the community—and with reality—than the ACLU.

They are right about one thing, however. There is going to be a concerted effort to smear this outstanding organization and it has already started. According to the same AP story, Levi Strauss & Company has dropped their support of the Boy Scouts of America. (Remember that fact when it is time to go back-to-school shopping, Mom and Dad.) Several United Way agencies have halted contributions to the organization (Remember that fact when the

United Way solicitation campaign begins, officer worker), and the state of Connecticut has removed the Boy Scouts from a list of state approved agencies that employees can support through payroll deductions.

An Atlanta newspaper columnist compared the Supreme Court decision to the Dred Scott decision of 1857, which affirmed the right of slavery. That is patently absurd. There is no comparison between the two decisions. One says a citizen has no right of choice. The other is all about choice. It is a fact so simple that it is baffling that others refuse to accept it. It is called free association. The fact that the organization doesn't want homosexuals as troop leaders is their right. This isn't new stuff, folks. This idea has been around a long time. I belonged to a fraternity in college. They chose me by the criteria they had established for membership. They certainly didn't ask me to approve the rules on whether I could belong or not. The same with a private club in Atlanta that accepted me as a member. They told me what the rules were. If I didn't agree, I didn't have to join.

What makes the Boy Scouts any different? They have a right to set their standards. If they choose only left-handed people for Scout leaders, more power to them. If you don't like their criteria, that is fine, too. Don't participate. It is a free country.

Rather than accept that fact, the special interests—and much of the media—want to insult the good name of the Boy Scouts of America even though the Supreme Court says they are within their legal rights to include or exclude whoever they choose. The smear campaign will fail. We are the "local community" that the ACLU so smugly predicts is going to walk away from the Boy Scouts. We won't turn our backs on them. The Scouts have done too much good for too long and they continually turn out outstanding young men. I am proud to say that two of my grandsons are Boy Scouts and they will be better for having been a part of scouting.

I applaud the organization for never wavering from their position. I think that is what sticks in the craw of the ACLU and gay rights groups. The Boy Scouts didn't blink on a matter of principle that was important to them. As a result, that principle is now the Law of the Land.

For once, the good guys won.

I Admit It!
I Worked
for ACOG!

Once again, I hear the siren call of corn-fried shrimp and am off to St. Simons Island and the exquisite little Georgia Sea Grill. I have decided if I am ineligible for heaven when I die—a likely possibility—I will accept St. Simons as second choice. I'm not sure I would know the difference. If they don't have corn-fried shrimp in heaven, St. Simons would be my first choice anyway.

Before I go, I beg your indulgence on a personal matter. A recent column suggesting that some 5000 boxes of Olympic junk be jettisoned rather than foisted off on taxpayers, as an Atlanta columnist proposed, precipitated an angry response from a Department of Public Safety bureaucrat. He accused me, among other things, of hiding the fact that I had worked for the Atlanta Committee for the Olympic Games and thereby having a vested interest in subverting the open records law. The writer "demanded" I admit my duplicity publicly. Otherwise, he would assume I had neither integrity nor ethics. Whether or not he could have me arrested for my alleged subterfuge he didn't say, but he seemed so overwrought that I figure before heading out onto the highways for my shrimp rendezvous, caution would dictate I go over this matter one more time. Otherwise, I may be eating C-rations in a county pokey.

Anybody that doesn't know I was with the Atlanta Committee for the Olympic Games has been on another planet for the past few years or manning a radar gun behind a billboard somewhere. I have referenced my association with the Olympics a number of times, including a few weeks ago when I announced I had written a book on the 1996 Games, due out in September.

Let me say, hopefully, for the last time: The matter of junking the boxes isn't an open records issue. The boxes have been available for public inspection since last July, including to the letter writer. When the Centennial Games were over, there were some 6000 boxes of paper. Outside experts went through them all and deemed 900 to be of historic value. The rest of the boxes contain worthless materials, including first aid forms, volunteer forms and the like. The Atlanta columnist who wanted all the boxes saved omitted the fact that taxpayers would end up footing the bill for the expense of carting off and storing the worthless material at the school or college of his choice.

Perhaps this further explanation will pacify the piqued public servant. The last thing I want is some state bureaucrat worrying about my integrity and ethics. It makes for inefficient government. However, if he is still not satisfied, I will be happy to give him the 5000 boxes and he can paper his house with first aid forms.

I wonder if Billy Payne ever regrets having brought the Olympic Games to Atlanta? Consider, for example, the Atlanta newspapers, which viewed ACOG like the Iranian ayatollahs view punk rock. Currently, they are combing the 900 boxes looking for materials with which to embarrass Payne. The last I heard they are going to make some insinuation about how tickets were distributed. No accusation of malfeasance, just another effort to demean the work of this good man. This, four years after the Games! Fortunately, they only succeed in making him more of a hero to the public and in making themselves look petulant and mean-spirited.

Know this, too: The Atlanta media, in their posturing and righteous indignation last year over the details of the Atlanta bid committee's efforts to win the 1996 Games, failed to note that their reporters were with the committee every step of the way in the bidding process. It is not that they didn't know what was going on. They did. They are just trying to cover their fannies.

This is why I wrote the book. I want to set the record straight on a number of issues. To date, you only know what you have read. Nobody has told you the other side of the story. We all know the media can dish it out. Now, we are going to find out if they can take it and still be objective. Just to be on the safe side, I have stored away a couple of extra barrels of ink. Frankly, I am looking forward to the fight.

Now, assuming I am back in the good graces of the anguished lawman, I am off to St. Simons. Look out, shrimp. Here I come!

Remembering the "Stealth Senator"

I don't know what I can say about Paul Coverdell that hasn't already been said except that I think he would be embarrassed by all the attention. Without question, he had the smallest ego of any politician I have ever been around.

I got to know him well during my days at the Atlanta Committee for the Olympic Games. One of my responsibilities was dealing with the federal government. The mantra in getting the Games to Atlanta was "no government funding." That meant that we would stage the Olympic Games with private dollars but, in fact, we needed a lot of government support "outside the fence." I was charged with getting the federal government to help us with security, transportation, housing, entry into and out of the country for some 15,000 athletes and officials from 197 countries, advanced weather forecasting and a myriad of other requests.

It wasn't an easy job by any measure but it could have been worse. The Clinton administration was anxious for good Games as they went into their reelection campaign, feeling a happy populace would likely vote for the status quo. The Speaker of the House was a Georgian who couldn't agree with the president on the time of day, but Newt Gingrich managed to put aside his differences with the White House on our behalf. With security our biggest need, we were fortunate to have Georgia Senator Sam Nunn to make our case in Congress and in the Department of Defense for the necessary personnel and materials.

And then there was Paul Coverdell. Without him, I don't know what we would have done.

Our chief critic was John McCain, the senator from Arizona. All the stories you have heard about his temper are not exaggerated. McCain had been infuriated a couple of years earlier when the World Cup was held in Los Angeles and the governing body had secured $50 million in government support. The games were a resounding financial success and the organizers celebrated by paying themselves huge bonuses and crediting the government's contributions for their personal good fortune. McCain went into orbit. Never again, he vowed, would the government provide support to such activities without getting reimbursed.

As luck would have it, we were next up and he decided to take out his World Cup frustrations on us. McCain constantly made serious, unsubstantiated and untrue charges about us constantly. His accusations weren't true but that didn't stop him from trying.

The only person able to deal with McCain was Coverdell. The Georgia senator's kind and patient demeanor belied an underlying toughness to take the intemperate McCain. But before bearding the lion, Coverdell would call us to his office to assure him that we were on track with our planning. His questioning was like that of a kind but stern schoolteacher. If you didn't have the answer, you had better go find it quickly. Once he was satisfied that we knew what we were talking about and he agreed with our approach, he would successfully face down McCain. How he did it, I'm not sure because I heard other senators express total frustration in trying to reason with the ill-tempered iconoclast. But McCain never bucked Coverdell.

As a result of being around Coverdell during and after the Games, my respect for him continued to grow. I called him the "stealth senator." He wasn't one to seek out sound bites and to appear on C-Span talking to an empty room. He preferred to know issues in great depth and then to quietly and effectively work behind the scenes to get things accomplished. He seemed to operate on the biblical injunction, "By his good works shall you know him." The Senate noticed. In his short time in Washington, he quickly moved up the ranks in the Republican leadership and was a close confidant of George W. Bush.

Coverdell was a rather formal man. I once invited him to attend the pre-Olympic diving competition. It must have been a hundred degrees. He showed up in a black pinstripe suit with shirt and tie and stayed through the whole competition without breaking a sweat.

I will truly miss this good man and our state will, too. I knew how much he was doing for us. It took his untimely death for everybody else to appreciate him.

The Revolt
Against
School Reform

August 14, 2000

It is time to dust off the metal detectors, groom the drug-sniffing dogs and crank up the heavy metal music. School is back in session! Time for the three R's: reluctant students, recalcitrant parents, and red tape.

After a year of meat-ax tinkering with our education system by the governor and the legislature, accompanied by grave nods of approval from business nabobs and howls of indignation from teachers' unions, many will claim this a new day for Georgia's public schools.

Close, but no cigar.

The new buzzword is "accountability." From now on, everybody in the educational environment is going to be held accountable for something by somebody. School boards. Principals. Teachers. Students. And on rare occasions, even parents. Cobb County, for example, has said they will issue fines to parents who don't show up for teacher conferences. Other systems are threatening parents who choose to keep their little darlings out of school until after Labor Day. Methinks we still have a slight problem with our schools.

Here is a further clue. Sometime back, I wrote a tongue-in-cheek column about getting a law passed in Georgia that parents would be held responsible for their children's actions. Some people caught the humor. Others were—to put it kindly—righteously indignant. They wanted me to understand the near impossibilities they face in raising children today. One even challenged me to publicly state how mine turned out. (They turned out fine, thank you, because of their mama, and they are raising their own kids that may turn out even better.) I heard every excuse in the book from that column and found them all wanting. Raising kids isn't all that hard. You love them and let them know that. You set fair and reasonable rules that everybody understands and you don't compromise those rules. The one thing that stresses children more than picking up their clothes is inconsistent rules. Finally, you keep the lines of communication open, which means you listen as much as you lecture.

Because this appears to be an impossible task for some parents, the intent seems to be to make the schools responsible for raising our kids as well as educating them. Many parents expect teachers to cram learning into their children's heads but won't get involved in the PTA because they are "too busy." Many parents don't show interest in their child's homework or, if they do, it is to criticize the teacher's assignments as irrelevant. And then there is a commonly held belief that says if the schools are forced to require prayer that the urchins will somehow turn into saints, allowing the rest of us to do as we please.

I give Governor Barnes an "A-Plus" for trying, but we are a long way from having our education problems under control. To do that, we are going to have to deal with drugs, poverty, single parent homes, latchkey kids, television trash, our penchant for suing every time something doesn't go our way and, most important, making excuses. Even King Roy can't make all of that go away.

In fact, I will make a prediction. There is going to be a backlash over the reforms being currently put in place. The changes that were wrought by the political and business forces over the objections of State School Superintendent Linda Shrenko and her allies were top-down and not well understood by rank-and-file citizens. I am hearing that dissent is beginning to bubble up from the grassroots as these new measures are implemented. Let me tell you about grassroots reactions. They scare the hell out of politicians because they can't be controlled. We have already seen some members of the legislature lose their seats as a result. We want simple solutions to complex problems and, alas, we haven't solved our public education problems with that single piece of legislative action last year.

If I thought I knew the answer, I would be shouting it from the rooftops. I have a strong vested interest in the issue. My son-in-law is a science teacher in Douglas County and was named Teacher of the Year last year by the *Atlanta Journal-Constitution*. In addition, my son has made a mid-career change and is at Kennesaw State getting a second Bachelor of Science degree and his teaching certificate.

I consider teaching a profession akin to ministry and medicine and am proud to have two educators in my family. Wish them—and all our teachers—luck. They are going to need it.

When Customers
Come in Second

Doesn't it warm you all over to know both Ford and Firestone consider us their Number One priority? About every 30 minutes, one of their CEO's is assuring us of that fact while they try to find out why Firestone tires and Ford Explorers seem to mix like oil and water.

Sorry, but I'm not buying their line. What is left out of their message is if we had been their Number One priority all along, the crisis might never have happened in the first place. Evidence will show, I predict, that someone made a decision somewhere along the way more focused on the bottom line than on the customer.

Now the debate centers on which tires in which plants were defective and was there enough psi in the tires and who is to blame. That's not customer focus. That is the bottom line talking again. If I owned a Ford Explorer or Firestone tires (I own neither), I would demand new tires regardless. My family deserves no less.

Unlike Ford/Firestone, I remember three crises where the customer's concerns really were put first. The most famous is the Tylenol case. Having found a bottle that had been tampered with, Johnson & Johnson pulled all the bottles off the shelf. Not just the ones made in certain plants or distributed to a certain area. They pulled all the bottles. Their quick action averted a disaster and a lot of lawsuits.

Then there was Chrysler. A number of years ago, it was reported that Chrysler executives were driving new cars a few hundred miles, turning back the odometers and selling the vehicles as new. Against legal advice, Chrysler chairman Lee Iacocca ran full-page ads with the headline, "We Goofed," and promising never to do that again. End of crisis.

Finally, there was the day that Coca-Cola executives Roberto Goizueta and Don Keough discovered we didn't want New Coke. We liked Old Coke. Much as Iacocca had done, Goizueta and Keough did a mea culpa and—marketing studies to the contrary—declared, "The customer is right. Give them back their Old Coke."

Despite these examples, companies don't seem to learn. They think words speak louder than actions and that we don't know the difference. We get these patronizing messages from corporations that seem to feel telling the whole truth is a crime against humanity. Call your typical company —any company—and get the maddening routine about punching touchtone buttons. How impersonal can you get? Then go read that company's annual report and particularly the CEO's message (he's the one with the halo over his head) about their all-day, everyday commitment to you, the customer. Bull feathers! The commitment is to the bottom line. Touchtone buttons cost less than people. You don't have to pay them benefits, buy them a desk, supervise them or hire and fire them.

Companies in all sectors are merging at alarming rates today. Yet, the mega-conglomerates assure us that there will be "more customer choice." Yeah right. In truth, customer choice is way down the list of reasons that companies merge. The bottom line is the first priority. CEOs get fired for poor financial performance, not poor customer service—unless poor customer service leads to poor financial performance.

Take airlines, for example. They cram us in like sardines— more fannies in seats mean more dollars to the bottom line—and then talk about their commitment to customer service. They know and we know there isn't a lot of choice as to which airline we can fly, so let's drop the bromides, please.

I am all for profit. I own stock in several companies and I cheer their financial progress on those rare days when they show any. But with 40 years of corporate hindsight, I suggest a company can be profitable and still not treat their customers as having no more sense than a hockey puck.

Early in my career I learned a rule about the external environment that is as inviolate as a law of physics. It should be the first thing taught in our business schools. Arthur Page, the first public relations vice president of AT&T, said more than 50 years ago, "All business in a democratic country begins with public permission and exists by public approval." That rule is as true today as when he said it.

Loosely translated, it means you and I still call the shots. Companies that ignore Page's rule do so at their peril. Ask Ford and Firestone.

Note to
M. Monchau:
"Butt Out!"

September 25, 2000

Pardon me if I am a little *grincheux* (That's French for "cranky") today, but I am more than offended that France's Atlanta-based consul general, Jean-Paul Monchau has decided to stick his *nez* (That's French for "nose") where it doesn't belong.

As a representative of the French government, his job should be to foster good relationships among *le Français* and *Les États Unis* but Monsieur Monchau seems to have a more important agenda. He wants the state of Georgia to declare a moratorium on capital punishment and states his intention of seeing that moratorium made permanent. He has put the *sauvage* (That's French for "ignorant hillbilly rednecks") on notice that his country is "firmly opposed to capital punishment, remains dedicated to its abolition and will continue to deeply deploy all its effort in that direction."

Let me say this *nettement* (That's French for "clear as a bell") to Monsieur Monchau: *Occupe-toi de ce qui te regarde.* (That's French for "Keep you damned nose our of our business.") I can't be more *nettement* than that.

It seems a part of the American culture to allow a bunch of pipsqueaks to tell us what is wrong with us as we wring our hands in shame. My daddy used to say, "You don't have to be smart; you just have to know who is smarter than you are." I don't find any of our critics doing a better job of running their country than we do in running ours. Yet the French, of all people, are criticizing the way we administer our law. Like a lot of people, I wonder from time to time whether capital punishment is morally right, but I don't need the Land of the Guillotine appointing itself our moral arbiter. If the French don't have enough to worry about, let me suggest they take a look at their own country. There are a lot of words that can be translated from French to English, but I don't think "work ethic" is among them. If there is even a suggestion of cutting back the 10-hour workweek and the 40 weeks of paid vacation in *Le Boondoggleville*, workers rush out and block all the highways, an exercise for which I assume they are being handsomely paid.

As I have watched the Japanese fumble and stumble through the Bridgestone/Firestone crisis, I am reminded of the number of meetings I attended in my corporate career where we agonized over the specter of the Japanese coming in and taking over our economy. In retrospect, that time could have been better spent learning to macramé. One meeting was devoted to an intense study of Honda's global strategy. It turns out that Honda's grand scheme was making engines and then finding things in which to put those engines, like lawn mowers and cars. I knew it was time for me to retire because that revelation failed to overwhelm me. You can put an engine in a fruitcake but you need to be able to market it, service it and build trust in it—something we do much better than the Japanese. While Ford doesn't deserve a gold star for the handling of its current crisis, they have done a damn sight better than Mitsubishi who hid customer complaints for 20 years.

We have people clamoring to get into the United States where the only thing that holds anyone back from achieving success is the amount of effort they are willing to expend. Once here, their first demand is that we learn their language. I don't want to learn their language. They need to learn English like the millions of immigrants who preceded them. Many countries require English in their schools because of the dominance of the language, but here the pressure is on us to learn the immigrant's language. Only in America—Land of the Free and Home of the Hyphen.

For some strange reason, we feel it necessary to self-flagellate as though we are embarrassed to be the wealthiest, strongest and most successful country on earth. We give money to everybody with a hand out—which includes most nations on earth—and then meekly accept their criticisms as proof of our own inferiority.

Well, I draw the line with Jean-Paul Monchau. If he doesn't like the way we run things in Georgia, I would suggest to him, *Il ne faut pas que la porte tel frappe en partant.* (That's French for "Don't let the door hit you on the way out.")

Au revoir!

News Media:
Enemy of
the People?

October 9, 2000

An Atlanta television cameraman is due in court in Haralson County in December to answer charges he provoked a group of black teenagers into burning a Confederate flag.

I hope there is nothing to the charge because journalists are already fast losing the American public's confidence. We don't need another body blow.

The First Amendment Center at Vanderbilt University has done a couple of extensive studies on public attitudes toward the media, and the results are unsettling. More than half the Americans surveyed last year—53 percent—said the press has too much freedom. ("Press" in this context includes broadcast media.) That is up 15 percent in just two years—a frightening trend.

But there's more. The survey indicates that most Americans believe newspapers should not be allowed to publish freely without government approval, that they should not be allowed to endorse or criticize political candidates, that journalists should not be able to use hidden cameras for newsgathering and that the news media should not be able to publish government secrets. That is downright scary.

A free press in a free country should never be popular. That is not our job. In a nation of checks and balances, the press is our most important check to ensure that institutions are operating in the people's interest. Last year, more than half the law enforcement agencies and school superintendents in Georgia who received requests from the media for public records refused to comply, according to the Georgia First Amendment Foundation. I guess they think the public's business is none of the public's business. That is why we must have a free press.

But the current negative attitude toward the media transcends the role of the press. It is *how* we do our job that seems to be the issue with the public.

In my opinion, the media are under siege for several reasons. First, there is so much competition for viewers and readers since the Internet has become a major news source that reporters are under greater pressure than ever to get the story first. This immediacy can sacrifice accuracy. I watched the media engage in a shameful feeding frenzy in 1996, trying to beat each other to the story of who planted the bomb in Centennial Olympic Park. They still got it wrong and almost ruined an innocent man in the process.

Second, the line between news and entertainment is blurring. We have had several instances in the past few years of television networks engaging in deceptive practices in pursuit of ratings. NBC surreptitiously blew up a GM truck trying to prove it was unsafe. ABC got caught rigging a piece on Food Lion stores. CNN ran a major story charging that U.S. troops fired nerve gas at defectors in Vietnam. It turned out to be untrue. The bottom line is a major loss of trust with the American public. That is why no one will dismiss out of hand the charges against the Atlanta television cameraman. Unfortunately, there is a precedent.

Third, I think too many media people operate on the premise that you are guilty until proven innocent. Having been on the other side of the fence, I found the press can be as arrogant as the institutions they are covering. I have endured lectures from young pup reporters on "their" first amendment rights until I reminded them the first amendment belongs to everybody, not just the press. Now the First Amendment Center survey notes the perception among Americans that free speech is more important than freedom of the press because, "freedom of the press belongs to the press while freedom of speech belongs to every individual."

Summarizing their survey findings, the First Amendment Center says there is "a real resentment of the press and its practices among Americans, who characterize the news media as arrogant, inaccurate, superficial, sensational, biased and bent. Worse, they apparently believe that the press is part of the problem, rather than part of the solution."

This is not good news for anybody. I am a newcomer to the media world, but I am also a citizen who depends on a fair, accurate and free press to keep me informed. The First Amendment Center study tells me a majority of Americans think we are doing a poor job. Who is to blame?

To quote that noted Okefenokee Swamp philosopher, Pogo the Possum, "We have met the enemy and he is us."

Sensitivity
Training for
Braves Fans? October 16, 2000

I hate to say "I told you so," but—well—I told you so.

For that small group of you who do not clip, paste and hermetically seal my columns each week, I predicted last April that the Atlanta Braves would fold like a cheap suit when October came. I had said it would be the Cincinnati Reds or the New York Mets that would do the Bravos in, but it was the St. Louis Cardinals who beat our local boys like a bass drum. Hey, I can't be right all the time!

Despite Atlanta having a pitcher who makes $5000 every time he throws a baseball sixty feet, six inches and a third baseman who earns at least that much every time he pffts a sunflower seed, the Cardinals roared through the Braves like Sherman through Georgia.

I saw it coming last spring when the management of the Atlanta Braves decided the team should undergo sensitivity training. In short, they took their eye off the ball. This bit of pandering was in response to ace reliever John Rocker's politically incorrect—but not factually incorrect—diatribe in a national sports magazine about New York City. Most anybody who has been to New York agrees with Rocker and even some of the native New Yorkers I've talked to said he was right but the PC police got him and held him until the black politicians and black preachers could jump his bones.

The Atlanta Braves historically have thumbed their noses at American Indians who find the tomahawk chop racially offensive but decided that keeping peace with the preachers and politicians was a lot more important than offending Native Americans. I guess because there are a lot more hell-raising black preachers and politicians in Atlanta than there are Indians.

So our bionic third baseman did make 25 errors this season. So our vaunted pitching staff got shelled like a bushel of peas in the playoffs. So our left fielder never saw a high fastball he couldn't swing at—and miss. At least they didn't offend any special interest group for 165 games. Way to go, guys!

What happens next year? Inside sources tell me that some serious changes are coming but not necessarily on the field. First, management, concerned about the high cost of attending the games, will make an extra effort to control costs. They will begin by pegging the price of bottled water to the world's gold standard, rather than platinum. Admittedly, that isn't much of a concession but it should get cost of water down into single digits. However, don't look for much of a change in the price of beer, hot dogs or popcorn. Nobody ever said getting kinder and gentler would be cheap.

Knowing that the public is fed up with the "close-but-no-cigar" performance of the team, the Braves are considering sensitivity training for fans as well next year. There is talk "The Star-Spangled Banner" may be shelved in favor of "We Are the World." No longer will you be subjected to some hip-hop version of our national anthem. Instead, fans and players alike will gather in the infield, hold hands and sway to this paean to brotherhood. I get cold chills just thinking about it.

My sources tell me that to ensure that nobody offends anybody anymore, the Reverend Timothy McDonald, head of the Concerned Black Clergy of Atlanta and leader of the assault on John Rocker, will sign a seven-year, $100 million contract, to pray before each game. I know what you are going to say: That is more money than Chipper Jones got but, hey, McDonald has had a better year. Just ask John Rocker.

With those measures in place, I would then suggest that the whole team find the Yellow Brick Road and follow it to Oz. Perhaps there, they can find a large dose of emotion. They seem to take great pride in their lack of it. But competitive athletics are all about emotion. Maybe the wizard can give them a little courage, too, to not cave in to special interest groups who use them for their own purposes. And if the wizard isn't too busy, maybe he could throw in another starting pitcher for good measure.

But hope springs eternal. It is only five months until a new season is upon us and we can start all over. There will be only one constant. The Braves will fold again.

I suggest you clip, paste and hermetically seal this column.

If You Don't Vote, Don't Whine

> *"The punishment which the wise suffer who refuse to take part in the government is to live under the government of worse men."* Plato (500 B.C. or thereabouts)

> *"Any able-bodied person who doesn't vote should be keel-hauled, dipped in boiling oil and forced to answer the mail generated by my column on Arab terrorists."* Yarbrough (2000 A.D.)

Power to the people! Once again, we choose the individuals to whom we will entrust the future of our country and ourselves. Once again, our federal government passes from one administration to another without bloodshed or revolt. It has been that way for over 200 years. But guess what? About half the registered voters in Georgia regularly skip one of the most important obligations we have as Americans—the right to vote. There is absolutely no excuse—none, zero, zilch, nada—for not voting. For those who could vote, but don't: Shame on you!

There are a lot of things about our country that need improving. There are a lot of things about the various candidates that need improving. There are a lot of things about democracy that need improving, but it is for damn sure that nothing will change if half the eligible voters sit on their behinds and refuse to get involved. Maybe these miscreants need to be shipped off to Rwanda or the Balkans or Afghanistan and see what happens when citizens cede power to the government. There you have no choice on who runs the country or how they run it and if you complain, you are liable to find yourself in some flea-bag prison, if you are lucky.

I was raised in a family that looked at voting as a sacred obligation. From the time they were eligible to vote until their last years, my parents cast their votes in person for every office from President of the United States to the East Point City Council. I'm not sure they ever voted absentee, feeling somehow this would weaken their obligation to pull the lever or mark the ballot. My first opportunity to vote was at the East Point City Auditorium when Dwight Eisenhower ran against Adlai Stevenson. I was expecting an epiphany or at least a bolt of lightning when I cast my vote. Actually, it turned out to be a pretty routine experience but nonetheless, it was neat to think this burr-headed kid was actually voting to elect the President.

Several years later, I skipped a Presidential election because I was playing tennis with some business associates and that seemed more important at the time. I happened to mention this to my dad later and felt like a heel when I saw his look. He didn't say anything but he didn't have to. He was clearly disappointed in me. I promised myself that I would never miss another election and I haven't.

Were my parents alive today, they would be shocked and saddened by the current state of voter apathy. I generally avoid using hard numbers in my columns because it interferes with my God-given ability to overstate, obfuscate and irritate but in a break with tradition, let me cite some statistics. Of people 18 years and older who are eligible to vote in Georgia, less than half did in 1996. Less than a third voted in 1998. Barely 50 percent went to the polls in 1992. Yet, in the past four years we have added almost 9 percent more eligible voters in Georgia. I ran these numbers through my trusty abacus and after carefully analyzing the results, determined we now have more people who find more reasons not to vote.

There is a silver lining to this cloud, however. Like the jungle, where strong animals kill off the weak ones so that future generations come from the best gene pools, perhaps the smart people vote while the dumb ones stay at home, eating their Twinkies and watching reruns of *Bay Watch*. That way, we don't weaken democracy's gene pool.

If you don't want to vote, that is your prerogative. A lot of Americans died to ensure you the right to be indifferent. But nobody gave their life for uninvolved whiners. If you don't vote, don't come running to me whining about inefficient and nonresponsive government and that "all politicians are crooked" and that "my vote wouldn't make a difference anyhow." No vote, no whining.

In fact, I wish my dad was around to hear your excuses. His look would make you want to crawl under a rock.

An Entire Year of Thanksgiving

Why set aside a single day to be thankful? If any people on earth should be constantly focused on our blessings, we are the ones. Therefore, by the power vested in me, I declare this Thanksgiving Year. I hope retail merchants don't take this as an excuse for a year-round Christmas selling season. Who wants to see Chia pets and electric foot massagers in July? But take all year—not just a day—to think about all that is good in your life.

I am thankful for health. Life is fragile. A bout of cancer six years ago should have taught me that, but two months after surgery, I was back at work dealing with issues I thought would mean the end of civilization as we know it. I have a hard time now remembering what those problems were.

I am thankful for family. I have a wonderful mate and two great kids who married well and produced four grandsons. It would require all of this page and most of the next to tell my grandsons what they have done for my life. It's true—grandchildren are the reward for having survived your children's teenage years.

I am thankful for my country. Somehow we have let patriotism fall out of favor and that is a shame. I grieve to see kids—and some adults—not remove their hat during the National Anthem. They should be forced to walk the cemeteries at Normandy and see what some people gave up so they could be disrespectful. I'm also tired of all the complaining about what is wrong with our country. We're doing just fine, thank you.

I am thankful I live in a state where "Georgia on My Mind" is the official song. (Can you imagine "Nebraska on My Mind"?) However, I would like to see a law passed that only Ray Charles or Willie Nelson may sing it. The song is too sacred to be placed in the hands of mere mortals.

I am thankful for Billy Payne, a decent man who did immeasurable good for our state by bringing the 1996 Centennial Olympic Games to Georgia. His reward was vilification by the Atlanta newspapers and a lack of gratitude from the snoots at the International Olympic Committee. History will treat him as a hero and his detractors won't even rate a footnote.

I am thankful for the people who do the little things we take for granted. They deliver our mail, pick up our trash, cut our grass, eliminate the strange noises in our automobiles and stop the leaks in our faucets. God bless them one and all.

I am thankful for the exquisite little Georgia Sea Grill on St. Simons Island. It is heaven on earth. The corn-fried shrimp isn't bad, either.

I am thankful for Wally Bunn and John Clendenin and Bob Holder and Jasper Dorsey, mentors all. They took a know-it-all and showed him he didn't know it all. My dad used to say that you don't have to be smart; you just have to know who is smarter than you. With these four, it is no contest.

I am thankful for loyal friends who encourage me when I need it and who stand with me in good times and bad. Why they care, I don't know. I am just grateful they do.

I am thankful for teachers—including the two in my family—police officers, fire fighters and emergency medical technicians. We don't pay them squat but, thank goodness, they give it their all.

I am thankful for my minister, Gil Watson. He makes you want to go to church. I just wish he would preach at least one sermon where I didn't feel like he was talking about me.

I am thankful for the University of Georgia. I can never repay my alma mater for all it has done for me. When I die, if I don't qualify for heaven—a real possibility—I will settle for Athens on a beautiful, crisp fall afternoon.

I am thankful for people who hold public office. The vast majority are honest, decent people trying to make a difference. We tend to lump them all with the few bad apples. That's not fair.

Finally, I am thankful for freedom of expression. I say what I believe and you tell me quickly whether or not you agree. I wouldn't have it any other way. It is called democracy.

The list is endless but not the space. Thank you.

How Not
to Can a
College Coach

Today, let us discuss the role of the chief executive officer, commonly referred to as the CEO. Our class assignment will be to look at the firing of Georgia football coach Jim Donnan and the role played by the University's CEO, Mike Adams.

The first thing to know about CEOs is they get paid the big bucks and find their pictures at the top of the organization chart because they are in charge. They are empowered—yea, required—to make decisions that no one else can or will make. If they make enough right decisions, they get paid more big bucks; if they don't, they have to move out of the big office with the plush furniture and find another job.

Having worked for a few CEOs in my past life, they all have one thing in common. They are decisive. You can't be in charge and not be decisive. CEOs are also human. They should make decisions based on the best advice they can get from people they trust. Unfortunately, too many surround themselves with loyalists who tell them what they want to hear or wait to be asked.

I must confess that President Adams did not consult with your humble servant before pulling the plug on Jim Donnan. My theory is that he understands my advice is worth what you pay for it: zero. However, that has never deterred me from freely dispensing it to one and all.

Had he asked, I would have told him he did the right thing for the football program. Friends who are intimately involved in the athletic program tell me that Donnan had lost control of the kids, both on and off the field. Another year wasn't going to change that.

However, I would not have let him do it the way he did. While CEO's do have responsibility for the ultimate decision, they should never get themselves—or allow others to get them in a position—where they can't delegate. As a result of the news conference, Mike Adams has established clearly that he is going to hire the new football coach. Therefore, he, not Athletic Director Vince Dooley, has just taken on the responsibility for the success or failure of that hire. That was a mistake. There is no crowd more fickle than the football crowd.

One thing that many CEOs have a hard time understanding is that perception is reality. Here is another dilemma for the University of Georgia. Over the past decade, UGA has grown into one of the finest academic institutions in the nation. We had finally tamed the football gods. Now, the president fires a guy who was 39-19 overall and 25-15 in the SEC. That isn't a bad record at most places but at Georgia, it gets the coach fired. Again, I support his decision but I would have told him to assure us all that the university is going to remain balanced between academics and athletics.

The news conference came off awkwardly—to be kind. Free advice: Always assume what the questions are going to be. Work out what the answers will be and who will respond. Get about three or four message points you want to make and make them over and over. There is no law that says you have to answer a question the way it is asked. You answer it like you want to. I don't think any of that was discussed prior to the press conference and, if it was, the execution resembled the Bulldogs on third and long—poor.

Vince Dooley looked as though he had been dragged to the table. He said too many times that he would have brought Donnan back for one more year. He should have said, "I support the president's decision. Our further discussions have convinced me it was the right decision." If he couldn't say that, he should have said, "I quit." Mike Adams, whether intentionally or not, made Dooley look bad. They did not look like a team. I would have counseled the president that Vince Dooley has more political clout in the state than he does.

There are tough days ahead for my university. How we fare is going to depend on the leadership of the CEO. What I saw at the news conference convinced me that Mike Adams is decisive and willing to take the heat. I just hope he is as willing to take advice. He is going to need it.

To My Grandsons: Thoughts on the New Millennium

January 8, 2001

To Brian and Thomas Yarbrough; Zachary and Nicholas Wansley:

Well, boys, it looks like we made it to the new millennium. Granted, the event was nowhere near as dramatic as Y2K, but it was pretty impressive nonetheless. The last time we did this was a thousand years ago and if we don't self-destruct the planet in the meantime, it will be another thousand years before we do it again.

You are fortunate to have lived through a change of centuries and then to have witnessed the start of a new millennium. When you think about all the people who have inhabited this earth since the beginning of time, you are in an elite group.

Who knows what the next millennium will bring? Or, the next century. Or even next year. Whatever happens, I am glad you live in this country.

If America took human form, it would be one giant hypochondriac. We are the most powerful nation on earth, but we whine and moan as though we are the sickest. We have lots of special interest groups that feed our angst because that is how they maintain their power. If they were to admit that things aren't as bad as they claim, they might have to fold their tents and get a real job. The fact is we are doing just fine.

Both your great-grandfathers were born early in the twentieth century, less than 100 years ago. Since that time, we have virtually eradicated once-fatal diseases like smallpox, tuberculosis, and polio. We have fought and survived two World Wars and two wars in Asia. We have become the most civilized, the best-educated and most technologically advanced nation ever to exist. We are also the wealthiest, the most humane—and the most insecure.

At your great-grandfathers' birth, we were just a half-century beyond the Civil War, which split the nation apart and inflicted wounds that lingered for many years. In retribution for the way we were treated in the aftermath of that war, we took it out on the people least able to defend themselves—poor blacks. Just as many Germans can't conceive of the Holocaust, it is hard to believe we once hung people simply because of the color of their skin. The rest we relegated to second-class citizenship until they finally got tired of it and rightfully demanded equal access to the American dream. Happily, most have taken advantage of the opportunity, and the result is a rapidly growing black middle class. From my observation of you and your friends, yours is the most color-blind generation yet and that gives me great hope for the future.

This is not to say that we don't have problems. We do. But for the life of me, I can't think of one country that doesn't. Most are too arrogant to admit it. Many of them resent our success. As a European friend once told me, "If America sneezes, the rest of the world catches cold," so we become a convenient excuse for other nations' stagnant economies, their internal strife and their lack of leadership. Rather than solve their own problems, it is easier to gather a bunch of thugs, invite the TV crews and burn our flag as we wring our hands, wondering what we did to deserve their displeasure.

In fact, we are the most caring and giving nation on earth, but it seems the more we care and the more we give, the more we are disliked. It is something we have to live with and, frankly, I haven't lost a lot of sleep over it. But be prepared for more of the same in the future. No country is dumb enough to take us head-on, but a lot of them will try to nibble away at our insecurities and, in turn, weaken our resolve. Don't let them do it.

I envy you. You have exciting times ahead of you. You can be whatever you choose and I hope you choose wisely. No matter what you do, do it to the absolute best of your ability. Don't cheat yourself or others by not giving your all. Try to leave the world better than you found it and keep a sense of humor. Laughter is good for what ails you. Finally, be proud that you are an American. We are the greatest nation on earth and deep down inside, we know it. Don't ever be apologetic about your good fortune.

Happy Millennium and much love,
Pa

Not My
Alma Mater's
Finest Hour

January 15, 2001

It was not my alma mater's finest hour.

Forty years ago this month, two young people who wanted to attend the University of Georgia along with other high school seniors in the state, were forced to go to federal court to gain admission. The two students were eminently qualified except for one extenuating circumstance. Both were black. As Federal Judge William A. Bootle so aptly stated in ordering their admission, the two "would already have been admitted had it not been for their race and color."

One of the students was Charlayne Hunter and the other, Hamilton Holmes. Hunter had finished third in her graduating class at Turner High School in Atlanta. Holmes had been valedictorian at Turner, as well as president of the senior class and co-captain of the football team. Although I had been graduated a couple of years before they applied, I must confess I had gotten in UGA with a record that paled in comparison to theirs.

As was the custom in those days, the university had balked at admitting the two black students and had earned itself a lawsuit. Ironically, one of the attorneys suing the institution on behalf of Hunter and Holmes was Horace Ward, who himself had been denied admission to the UGA law school a decade earlier.

Getting into the University of Georgia was one thing. Staying there was quite another.

Just three days after arriving, Hunter was greeted at her dorm by a mob hurling bottles, bricks and profanities before being dispersed by police and the legendary dean of men, William Tate. (No student protesting any issue—including the integration of the University of Georgia—would have dared challenge Dean Tate. He was a giant of a man.) Holmes and Hunter went back to Atlanta while tempers cooled down on campus. It took another court order, an expression of concern by some 400 UGA faculty members, and a rare show of courage by state political leaders to get them back in school to stay.

In 1963, both Hunter and Holmes were graduated from the

University of Georgia. Hunter began a journalism career and Hamilton Holmes, who had been elected to Phi Beta Kappa, received his medical degree from Emory University and became an orthopedic surgeon.

It is a far different and much better university that recently commemorated the fortieth anniversary of the desegregation of the institution. As a part of the ceremony on campus, the landmark Academic Building was appropriately renamed the Holmes-Hunter Building. Included on the program were former Governors Ernest Vandiver and Carl Sanders. It was in part because of these men that Georgia opted to do the right thing and shun the race-baiting—and futile—tactics of George Wallace in Alabama and Ross Barnett in Mississippi. Forty years later, we are still trying to do the right thing. Now, however, the University of Georgia is under legal attack for trying to be more inclusive, not less. Go figure.

I have never met Charlayne Hunter (now Hunter-Gault), but I got to know Hamilton Holmes well when we served as trustees on the University of Georgia Foundation. I was the better for it.

I found a quiet, self-effacing person who seemed to bear no ill will for what we had put him through some two decades earlier. In that way, he reminded me of another great man, Andrew Young, who was on the front lines of the civil rights movement and came out the other side of that maelstrom as loving of his fellow human beings as when he entered.

Like Young, Hamilton Holmes suffered the slurs, the insults, the meanness, and the hypocrisy of "separate but equal" with dignity, class, and courage and showed us that he was bigger than his enemies. Like Young, he should forever serve as a role model to both blacks and whites instead of the current crowd of race-mongers who seem intent on dividing us instead.

I just wish my friend could be here to observe the progress his university has made. He would be pleased. While he would be loath to take credit, his bravery helped change the course of history in the state of Georgia. Unfortunately, Hamilton Holmes died in 1995 at the age of 54. It was much too early.

I believe that we should all leave this world better than we found it. Many of us try. Most of us fail. A few manage to do it. Hamilton Holmes was one of those people.

I am privileged to have known him.

One Less
Airline to
Kick Us Around

Take heart, O weary traveler. There will soon be one less airline to kick you around. American Airlines has announced plans to take over TWA. Just what we need in the airline industry—less competition!

The news gets even better. Donald Carty, American Airlines CEO, says less competition will actually benefit the flying public. With two national airlines—American and United—you will be able to go anywhere in the country and the two mega carriers will fall all over themselves to convince you to fly with them. Yeah, right. Maybe I missed this part, but I don't remember him saying anything about less competition making flights more affordable, seats more comfortable, food more edible, or personnel more customer-friendly.

If we follow his logic, then Continental should take over Northwest (who doesn't fly when it snows). They would then merge with Delta (who doesn't fly when its pilots are mad, which is most of the time), who would merge with United or American, who would then take over each other. With that accomplished, the whole crowd would then merge with AOL/Time Warner/Turner/Looney Tunes. Now you are talking some serious customer benefit!

Don't scoff at Carty's claims too quickly. He might be right. Maybe things will get better if one of the airlines disappears. They can't get much worse. Example: This past Christmas, a friend's son who lives in Washington came to Atlanta for the holidays. He had only a short time to visit, so rather than risk delays or cancellations, he took the train!

One of the main benefits of semiretirement is that I don't have to fly much anymore. For nine years, I had a staff in Washington and a lot of business in New York and flew almost weekly. Looking back on that experience today, I don't know how I survived. I read somewhere that animals have some kind of chemical in their body that renders them numb before they are killed by other animals. That way, they don't experience the pain. I am convinced that airline travelers have that same chemical. I could always tell the rookie flyers. They would let their frustrations boil over when something didn't go right and rip into flight attendants, gate agents or skycaps. Kind of like a chihuahua barking at a water buffalo. After a few more flights, you would see these same people with eyes glazed and heads down, slowly shuffling through the airport. Clearly, the chemical had kicked in and they no longer felt the pain. The airlines had claimed another victim.

Back in the late '70s, I had a tour of duty with AT&T in Washington when deregulation was all the rage with Congress. The Bell System knew that trucks and airlines would be deregulated first and then would come telecommunications. One of my responsibilities was to monitor the progress of airline deregulation. As I sat and listened to the bureaucrats and economists and think tank pointy-heads extol the virtues of competition in the airline industry, I vividly recall Senator Fritz Hollings, of South Carolina, predicting that as soon as they were cut free of regulation, airlines would cease serving the small markets and chaos would ensue. He was more right than wrong with his prediction.

Airline deregulation has more people flying—although I believe that would have happened with or without deregulation—but airlines have been unwilling or unable to accommodate the increased traffic and have lost the loyalty of the public as a result. Look no further than our own back yard and see what has happened to Delta Airlines. Delta squeezes more people into smaller seats, cuts amenities—but not prices—and tries to live off its reputation from the days when there was a genuine love affair between the airline and its customers. Despite the best efforts of a lot of good people on the front lines, today's Delta ranks in popularity somewhere between Tammy Faye Bakker and the Internal Revenue Service.

If you have to travel, you have little choice but to fly. You endure the delays, the cancellations, the cramped space, the stressed employees and all the other unpleasantness of air travel or you stay home. Take it or leave it.

But with the American Airlines takeover, look for things to improve dramatically in the airline industry. The planes will be roomier, the personnel enthusiastic, and you will arrive at your destination on time, every time.

If you believe that, I have a bridge in Brooklyn to sell you.

A Case
of Bad Gas

Before being allowed to correspond with you on a regular basis, I was required to recite the Columnist's Oath. In doing so, I solemnly swore I would uphold the Constitution of the United States, defend it against all enemies, domestic and foreign, never use words like "synergy" and "input," and read my thesaurus every day. I also pledged to take complicated issues and explain them in such a simple way that you would feel compelled to clip and paste for future reference.

Today my topic is the deregulation of natural gas in the state of Georgia. This seems to be a matter of some interest since a number of you are contemplating selling your firstborn to pay for the privilege of not freezing to death.

The idea of deregulating natural gas began in the offices of the Georgia Public Service Commission. The commissioners were sitting around one day lamenting the fact that although they are elected statewide, nobody knows who they are. Gone are the halcyon days of Bobby Pafford and Billy Lovett when the PSC was battling utility rate increases and hearing rooms were filled with consumer advocates, lawyers and lots of television cameras.

"I have an idea," said one commissioner, "let's reform public education." "That is not in our jurisdiction," said a second commissioner. "Besides, Roy Barnes has already beaten us to it." Then a third commissioner—who will go nameless to protect his well-being—leapt from his chair and cried, "Eureka! I have it. Let's get the Legislature to deregulate natural gas in Georgia. We will become famous for being the first state to deregulate the utilities. Songs will be written about us. Our children's children will read about us in history books and we will all be reelected by acclamation."

"Not so fast," cautioned a fourth. "California has already deregulated their utilities and their politicians are basking in the glory of their success." "A mere technicality," sniffed his colleague. "They only deregulated electric utilities. We are talking natural gas. Nobody in Georgia cares what happens in California. Our electorate will be in awe when we take credit for being first. We will be so popular we'll have to take turns being governor."

Thus it was that natural gas deregulation was born.

As a first step, the local monopoly, Atlanta Gas Light, agreed to haul the gas in from Texas or Louisiana or Cleveland—wherever the stuff comes from—and to form a marketing company that would compete with the host of other companies that eagerly sought to provide natural gas to the homes and businesses in the state. The PSC wanted customers to have a variety of choices and they got it—from large companies like SCANA and Georgia Natural Gas to entrepreneurs like Manny's Sump Pump Repair. Alas, many of the marketers quickly fell by the wayside. They have no one to blame but themselves. These companies made the strategic error of billing their customers every month and thus severely impacted their bottom line. The savvy marketers only billed customers when they got around to it—which was mostly never—and saved additional dollars by including in the first bill, notice to discontinue service for nonpayment of all the other bills they had not sent.

As the Public Service Commission had hoped, there has been little reaction from the general public to natural gas deregulation. Many users have no idea what they are being billed for and therefore can't figure out what questions to ask. A large number are too cold to care and the rest are too busy researching which commissioner is next up for reelection.

Once again, the state of Georgia has stepped out front. We showed those Chardonnay-drinking liberals in California a thing or two. Our natural gas deregulation effort is the envy of the rest of the country. Admittedly, the other states don't seem to be rushing to emulate our success, but that is because they are too jealous to admit our utility commissioners are smarter than theirs.

As for California, it won't be long until their lights go out and they come hat in hand, begging us to sell them some of our natural gas. We'll do it but just to rub it in, we won't send them a bill.

With that, dear reader, I trust I have fulfilled my oath and have explained to your satisfaction why the Georgia Public Service Commission chose to give us all a bad case of gas. Please clip and paste.

Roy's Hand
Firmly on
the Throttle

Harry Truman said, "If you can't stand the heat, get out of the kitchen." In case you haven't noticed, Roy Barnes has the burners going full blast and hasn't even broken a sweat. You are witnessing one of the most politically astute, bright, active, gutsy governors in our state's history—and he isn't even through his first term!

I make a lot of speeches around the state and for the past year, I have been telling audiences that the state flag was political dynamite—too hot to handle until after reapportionment. I predicted Governor Barnes would have a tough time getting the Legislature to change the current flag because of pressure the legislative leadership—many of whom are from middle and south Georgia—would feel from constituents opposed to the change. While I was pontificating, the governor was quietly putting together his plans to change the flag. He blew it by the opponents—and me—so fast that nobody saw it coming. I can't recall a more potentially divisive issue being managed with more political skill than Roy Barnes' handling of the state flag. You may not agree with the decision but you have got to admire the precision with which he got it done.

Now, of course, the losers are vowing revenge at the polls, which is their right, but they are wasting their time. In truth, the only person who can beat Roy Barnes is Roy Barnes. Too many CEOs surrounded themselves with people who are afraid to tell their leader the truth. When you have had as much success as Barnes has, it is easy to start believing in your invincibility. I trust his advisers like chief of staff Bobby Kahn won't let that happen to their boss. Hopefully, they learned a lesson with their heavy-handed "my-way-or-the-highway" approach to education reform last year. In their effort to do the right thing, they angered a lot of hard-working teachers and, as a result, caught the flak they deserved.

The thing that impresses me most about Governor Barnes is his willingness to take on the complex and politically unattractive quality of life issues that our rapid expansion has brought us over the past two decades. While we can hyperventilate over what the new flag looks like—and it looks ugly as a pig to me—our future rides on more substantive issues, like getting our state's transportation problems under control, cleaning up the air we breathe, spreading development around the state and insuring that we have enough water to support the current and anticipated growth in our state. There is no city or county in the state with the resources or political will to solve these problems individually. It is going to take the strong hand of Roy Barnes.

Barnes has that hand firmly on the political throttle. He managed to keep both urban black and rural white Democrats together and got the flag changed. He is helped immeasurably by a Republican leadership in the Legislature that can't find their backside with both hands. Example: Republicans were told by their leaders to stay away from the flag issue and let the Democrats handle it themselves. They did. It was the political equivalent of asking the fox to guard the henhouse.

Georgia has been blessed with a string of able, honest governors going back to Ernest Vandiver. Prior to that, we had the powerful Talmadge political machine that dictated just about everything that happened in the state. Roy Barnes is a combination of both. He has been in politics for almost a quarter of a century with no questions of impropriety and has amassed more power in his three years in office than any governor since Gene Talmadge.

I hear people say that Barnes will have a tough reelection given the anger of pro-flag proponents and the residual resentment in the educational establishment. Forget it. Roy Barnes will easily win a second term. The large majority of Georgians like what they see in the governor's office—someone willing to take on tough issues and make things happen.

Chances are that Governor Barnes is going to experience a few bumps in the road in his second term, particularly if our economy falters and expansion slows. If that happens, his detractors will be on him like white on rice, hoping to even the score on a number of issues, including the state flag. They won't have far to go to find him. He will be in the kitchen—enjoying the heat.

Losing Our
Drawl —
and Our Charm

February 26, 2001

I don't know about you, but I am not exactly dancing on the rooftops over the 2000 census. According to the nose counters at the Census Bureau, Georgia is now the tenth-largest state in the union. Our population grew from 6,478,216 in 1990 to 8,186,453 in 2000, an increase of 24.6 percent. This growth reminds me of something my wise father once said. Daddy opined that the state wasted a lot of money painting stripes down the middle of the road. Nobody ever went north. They all came south.

I haven't been able to analyze the census numbers in great detail yet because I have been too busy reorganizing my sock drawer, but I have a sneaking suspicion that of the 1,708,237 who came to Georgia in the last decade, 37 came from Alabama and Mississippi. The other 1,708,200 came from Guatemala, Hanoi, Cleveland, Newark, Detroit, and New York City. Of that number, 1,000,000 brought preconceived notions that we are a bunch of rednecks who live on dirt roads and marry our cousins.

We are just going to have to learn to adjust. We could start by not continuing to fight the Civil War, known to some as the War of Northern Aggression. The last time I checked the history books that unpleasantness had ended about 136 years ago. We lost. You keep bringing it up to the newcomers and they will keep telling you how their great-grandfathers kicked our great-grandfathers' butts. It is bad enough that I have to listen to my UGA compatriots continue to talk about losing three in a row to Georgia Tech, but why keep reminding everybody that we came in second in a two-country war?

The chamber of commerce won't tell you this, but the crowd that showed up over the past decade didn't come cheap. We had to build more roads, import more gasoline, bulldoze more land, open more strip malls, install more red lights, suck up more water and foul more air.

Alas, there is something at work here even more serious than finding room for a bunch of snowbirds. If this in-migration keeps up at its present rate, we risk losing our unique Southern heritage. We must stay ever vigilant or it won't be too long before our barbecue joints with sawdust on the floors and Willie Nelson on the juke box will be replaced by sushi bars and waiters named Greg, telling us to have a nice day. Pickup trucks will be supplanted by SUVs. Yard dogs by poodles. High school football by ice hockey and sweet tea by microbrewed beer. Some of this I can live with. But I draw the line at losing our lilting, honey-smooth Southern drawl. We seem to have some kind of inferiority complex about the way we speak. Maybe that is because our friends from north of the Mason-Dixon line take great delight in tweaking us about our "slow talking," as though slow speech equates to slow thinking. Guess what? We aren't too dumb. We didn't move north, did we? Besides, what is so intelligent about "fuhgedabowdit"?

One more census like that last one and you might never again hear words like "ranch" ("Honey, would you hand me my ranch? Ah'm gonna tighten the bolts on the pickup") or "far" ("Ah luv you so much, my heart's on far") or "bard" ("Your no-good brother just bard my last dollar") or "thank" ("Ah thank ah'll have a Co-Coler")

Fortunately, we dodged a bullet this time. Two-thirds of the newcomers settled in the Metropolitan Atlanta area, and Atlanta isn't Georgia. In fact, Atlanta has about as much in common with Georgia as butter does with butterfly. Atlanta has always wanted to be like New York City and got its wish. Now everybody in Atlanta drives too fast, eats sushi and watches ice hockey.

So take heart, Hahira. Rejoice, Roopville. Celebrate, Cedartown. The fact that all these folks decided to congregate in Atlanta over the past ten years means that you can crank up Willie Nelson in the pickup as loud as you want, drive to your favorite barbecue joint as slow as you want, and eat chitlin cornbread and drink sweet tea as much as you want. But let me give you some advice. Don't go around bragging about how good you've got it. Otherwise, when they finish counting us in 2010, you may find Greg serving you raw fish and telling you to have a nice day. That would ruin everything.

Return to Reality— and Delta

March 5, 2001

I have just returned from a tour of Australia and New Zealand. I didn't want to go, but as is usual in my household, we took a vote. The final tally was 1-1. I lost.

If you are planning to go Down Under, let me warn you, it is a long way from here. To get there, you must cross the international dateline. That means it is always tomorrow in Australia. That excited me because I figured I would know the latest news before it ever happened. For example, if Sam Nunn and Ted Turner and their Nuclear Threat Initiative were successful in disarming Barbados, I would know it first. If the Rainbow Coalition named Jesse Jackson, "Father of the Year," I would know that, too. If Bill Clinton insisted that he really didn't mean to pardon Marc Rich but in the last-minute rush to pardon Charles Manson, the Chicago Black Sox and Judas Iscariot, somebody sneaked Rich's name in the pile, I would have had knowledge of that long before anyone else, except maybe Hillary.

Alas, it did not work that way. Even though it is tomorrow in Australia, they think it is today. Therefore, the only news I got was how their cricket team can't seem to beat India—doesn't that take your breath away?—and how the Labor Party is about to take power from the ruling Liberal Party—or maybe it is the other way around.

I did learn a few things, though. Although my tour group hailed from both coasts and every place in between, I found that good people live all across America. We had more in common than we had differences. Politicians need to get out of the beltway and talk to folks like these and discover what they are thinking instead of being held captive by special interest groups. They just might learn something themselves.

I learned to appreciate the environment more after seeing New Zealand. This is perhaps the most beautiful country on earth and must be what the U.S. looked like before we discovered strip malls, parking lots and fast food. The only thing more impressive than the landscape was the people. They are genuinely nice. We need to import them over here to teach us how to deal with customers.

I learned that no matter how nice we try to be, Americans are intimidating. As I discovered in my travels with the Olympics, we are viewed as rich, aggressive and clueless as to what is going on in the rest of the world. That is not a totally inaccurate appraisal.

Regrettably, after two weeks of spectacular scenery, great food and wonderful camaraderie, it was time to cross the international dateline and return to today. I came home to find nothing had changed while I was gone. Our natural gas bills are still higher than the gross national product of Czechoslovakia, and the legislature and the Public Service Commission are scrambling to cover their backsides over this debacle. Frankly, it bothers me that the PSC has entrusted its chairmanship to a guy named Bubba McDonald. I have always been uncomfortable giving a lot of responsibility to anybody named Fats, Hoss or Bubba.

But I really knew it was business as usual when we arrived in Los Angeles and prepared to board Delta Airlines for the trip home. Our tour of Australia and New Zealand had required us to fly seven different times on either Air New Zealand or Ansett Australian Airlines. Each flight was near perfect, on time with friendly personnel and edible food. Quite a contrast to the surly Delta flight attendant we endured en route to LA, but nothing compared to the return trip. Our first flight was cancelled and the next flight was an hour and a half late leaving. (Some of the delay was the result of Delta having sold four tickets to two seats on an otherwise full flight.)

I think Bubba and the guys handling natural gas deregulation are beyond help but I have the perfect solution for Delta. Arthur Blank has announced his retirement as CEO of Home Depot. He has a lot of money and now he will have a lot of free time. Perhaps we can prevail on him to buy Delta and instill some of the Home Depot culture in the airline—low prices and a strong customer orientation. Besides, I think the pilots would look great in those orange aprons.

It's nice to be home.

How Courts
Failed to
Serve Justice

March 26, 2001

I am suffering from a bad case of contempt of court. The sources of my contempt are Fulton County Superior Court Judge Alice Bonner and convicted murderer Ronald Keith Spivey.

In case you missed it, Judge Bonner recently dismissed a hit-and-run-case because two attorneys from Howard's office were 15 minutes late. The legal beagles thought they were supposed to be there at 9:30 A.M. The judge said they were supposed to be there at 9 A.M. Case dismissed. I guess Her Eminence had never heard of fining lawyers for being late or putting their fannies in jail or buying them a Mickey Mouse alarm clock. When you are in a snit, you tend to overlook those little details.

The case in question concerned Shareca Tucker, killed in November 1998 when struck by four cars while crossing a road in suburban Atlanta to catch a bus for work. One of those charged with hit-and-run was Rosendo Abarca. He was the beneficiary of Her Omnipotence's ruling. Abarca's lawyer, George Handelsman, says his client thought he had hit some debris or had gotten a flat tire so he left. Like a lot of lawyer blather, I take that with a grain of salt but, sadly, we don't know what the truth is because Her Worthiness decided to chuck the whole thing.

Now, she has issued the judicial equivalent of an "Oops!" and says Abarca should be tried after all. She even suggested some other judge should hear the case, which is the first thing she has said that has made sense since the whole unfortunate mess began. There is just one teeny-tiny problem. We have a constitutional prohibition against being tried twice for the same crime. It is called double jeopardy. Unless Mr. Handelsman got his law degree from Fred's U-Haul and Motorcycle Repair, I suspect he will fight any attempt to have his client tried again. We could be talking about years.

Nowhere in this whole sorry episode does anyone seem to have considered the feelings of Shareca Tucker's mother, Sharon Brownlee. Because the lawyers and a judge couldn't agree on what time to get to work and now whether to even have a new trial, she has been denied the opportunity for closure of a very personal and painful event in her life. I wonder how Ms. Brownlee feels about our justice system today?

Civil libertarians and other assorted do-gooders are quick to grab television face time to talk about defendants' rights. How about a little concern for the victims' families? Don't they have some rights, too? At the same time that Ms. Brownlee was enduring the ridiculous spectacle in the Fulton County Superior Court, wondering if her daughter's case will ever come to trial or if will be deep-sixed by clever lawyering and poor judging, the rest of us were enduring the public hand wringing on behalf of Ronald Keith Spivey.

Spivey was convicted of murdering Columbus police officer Billy Watson almost 25 years ago. In case you're counting, that is a quarter of a century. He was scheduled for electrocution. Now, there is a question as to whether or not electrocution violates the Eighth Amendment, prohibiting cruel and unusual punishment. I wonder if that same amendment applies to Officer Watson's family? A bunch of preachers are petitioning the courts to prohibit electrocution because it subjects the inmates to "severe pain and prolonged suffering." Funny, Reverends, but that same line of reasoning could apply to the family of Billy Watson and to Sharon Brownlee.

Why don't some of the do-gooders look at the grief and agony that we have put these people through? Why don't they take their candles and go stand in front of the Watson house and sing, like they will whenever we get around to deciding how to get ol' Ronnie Keith a one-way trip to visit his Maker? Why doesn't Judge Bonner tell Sharon Brownlee she blew it big time?

Our system of justice is supposed to be blind, as in not favoring one side over the other. Call me naïve, but I think in the cases of Shareca Tucker and Billy Watson, Lady Justice has been peeking out from behind her blindfold and stacking the deck against the victims. That is what I find so contemptible.

In the meantime, should someone send the deputies to arrest me for contempt of court, I will be easy to find. I will be the one holding my nose because this kind of justice stinks.

The Logic
of Half-Brain
Thinking

April 23, 2001

Here is some news that is going to knock your socks off.

A bunch of researchers at Indiana University School of Medicine who had too much time on their hands—and probably too much government money—have made a startling discovery. They have determined through some scientific mumbo-jumbo that men listen with only half their brains, while women use both sides.

Where have these folks been? They could have found out the same thing with a simple phone call to my wife. She would have confirmed that men not only don't listen, if they are using even half a brain that is the equivalent of full throttle.

My mate is a recognized expert on such matters because she has been conducting her own study on male habits for a number of years and her results cover a wide variety of topics, not even broached by the whizzes in Indiana.

For example, men listen with only half a brain because women only talk to men when (a) they are trying to read the paper, (b) watching Tiger Woods hit a hook shot around a tree and over water to a tiny green to force a playoff or (c) Frank Sinatra is singing "My Way."

When we do tune in, we find that women only want to talk about the fact that they have nothing to wear on vacation, which is eight months away.

My wife's study has uncovered a number of other fascinating facts about men. For example, no red-blooded male would dare ask directions under any imaginable circumstance. Genetically, we are explorers. We will eventually find the place we are looking for because we can tell from the location of the sun whether we are going east or west, north or south. Women are incapable of such precise reckoning and must resort to either using a road map or making us stop the car to ask a 7-11 clerk. It is the quitter's way. My wife's only defense—and it is a weak one—is that we have never, ever been to Macon that we didn't get totally lost. While that may be true, we have seen parts of Macon that even the natives don't know exist. That is why guys like Lewis and Clarke were successful. Explorers don't rely on 7-11s.

Her study also reveals that men don't use plates when eating, especially while watching television. We have this innate sense of how long the commercials are going to last and we can make it to the kitchen, fix a sandwich, grab some milk, chips and a few cookies and be back in our seat just as the car commercials fade and John Wayne reappears. This does not allow time to open the cupboard and get a plate. Her study concludes men should eat at the table. My own independent research refutes that. When suddenly seized with a case of the munchies, I can usually reach into the crevices of my chair and pull up a goodly number of peanuts, popcorn or pretzels. It is the same God-given survival technique as squirrels storing nuts for later use. Because she doesn't watch the nature shows on PBS, this concept is totally lost on her.

Another handicap of having only half a brain is that men can remember how many home runs Hank Aaron hit (755) and the longest consecutive major league hitting streak (Joe DiMaggio hit safely in 56 straight games) and the last man to hit .400 (Ted Williams, .406, 1941), but we can't remember to wipe our feet when we come in the house or to turn off the lights when we leave the room or Valentine's Day.

As if women needed any more reasons to feel superior, the Indiana University study showed that because women use their whole brain, they can listen to more than one conversation at the same time. Big deal. What is so great about using your whole brain to listen to two other women talk simultaneously about how their husbands forgot Valentine's Day?

So maybe we guys are half-brains. That doesn't bother me at all. While my whole-brain wife is deliberating about what to wear on next year's vacation, I am going to sit back and watch Tiger hit that magical shot as I munch on the month-old pretzel I found under the seat cushion. I will also be trying desperately to remember where we are going on vacation. If she told me, I guess I wasn't listening.

The President
and the Payout

This is a column I wish I didn't have to write.

I consider the University of Georgia as family. I have served as president of the national alumni society. UGA has named me their outstanding alumnus. I have a facility named for me in the College of Journalism. I give my time and my dollars to the institution. I bleed red and black. But today I am not happy with my university.

Bill Shipp, Georgia's veteran political observer, recently reported that in the summer of 1998, Mike Adams, president of the University of Georgia, made a secret deal to pay head football coach Jim Donnan an additional $255,250 if he was terminated before his contract expired. It seems that Donnan's agent, Richard Howell, wasn't getting anywhere in his negotiations with the coach's boss, Athletic Director Vince Dooley, so he decided to bypass everybody and go to the top. The top is Adams, the CEO.

Somehow Jim Nalley, who was chairman of the UGA Foundation board of trustees (of which I am a member) at the time and who to my knowledge had no reason to be dealing with athletic department matters, got involved and a deal was made with Howell. The three of them then decided that neither Dooley nor the athletic board, which has governance on such issues, should know of the agreement.

Had Wayne Clough, Georgia Tech's president, done what Adams did, I would have nailed my friends at North Avenue before the ink was dry on Shipp's column. Because it was my beloved UGA and because Adams, Nalley, Dooley and Shipp are my friends, I tried to ignore the episode but I couldn't. Frankly, I didn't like what was done and I didn't like the way it was done.

I don't know a lot about a lot of things but I know a good bit about working with CEOs because I spent most of my past life doing just that. CEOs get their jobs because are smarter than everybody else. They are also decisive. CEOs must make decisions that no one else is empowered to make. Because they are smart and decisive, they can be intimidating. They are prone to think themselves invincible and they are not. That is why they need good people around them giving them sound advice, whether they want to hear it or not. Good advice begets good decisions. Bad advice begets bad decisions. No advice begets secret deals with sports agents.

Mike Adams either did not share with his staff what was going on or they were reluctant to tell him this was a very bad idea or maybe Jim Nalley, a prominent alumnus, pushed him to make the deal. Whatever the reason, any student in Public Relations 101 would have counseled Dr. Adams not to do what he did. You don't make secret deals at public institutions like the University of Georgia. In the first place, it is not right. In the second place, these things always have a way of becoming public and careening out of control. You also don't bypass your chain of command, in this case Vince Dooley. That is bad for morale.

A couple of years ago, Dr. Adams announced suddenly that he was planning on changing the structure of the journalism college. The reaction from alumni and faculty was so severe he had to back down. "Why," I asked one of his staffers, "didn't he talk to some influential alumni ahead of time? He might have gotten their support had he done so." The response was that "he was just exercising his power as president."

None of his advisors seems willing to tell him, so let me bite the bullet. The only power President Adams has is what is bestowed on him by the constituencies he serves: students, faculty, alumni, donors, the Board of Regents, the General Assembly, the governor, taxpayers and so on. The University of Georgia belongs to all of the above. We have entrusted the institution to him to operate on our behalf and in the open.

I am a strong supporter of Mike Adams and appreciate his willingness to take on the tough issues that pop up in academia like kudzu. He has one of the toughest jobs in the state, but he made it much harder than it should be by his clandestine agreement with the agent of a football coach he would later fire.

That was dumb as dirt and somebody should have told him that before now.

Open Letter to My Son, the Teacher

May 14, 2001

To my son, Ken:

I have been proud of you since the day you were born but never more so than right now. After almost 20 years in the business world, you are about to become a teacher. When you step up on the stage at Kennesaw State University and get your teaching certification, it will be one of the great moments in my life.

There are four professions that rank above all others: religion, medicine, education and public safety. All four touch humankind in unique ways: Religion cares for the soul; medicine, the body; education, the mind; and public safety, our ability to live peacefully with one another. To do these jobs well requires a passion and commitment far beyond what is expected of the rest of us.

This is an interesting time for public education in Georgia. Governor Barnes has placed education reform as the centerpiece of his administration. We could make his efforts a lot easier if we truly cared about having better schools. We say we care, but sometimes I wonder. It is like highway safety. We all say we want safe roads but then we drive like idiots.

You will find everybody seems to be an authority on how our children should be educated. Politicians think if you throw money at public education, it will solve all the problems. Special interest groups resist any efforts to change the status quo, even though it would make for a better learning environment because they fear losing power and influence. Nonsupportive parents expect you to raise their children for them and then give you hell if you try to apply a little discipline. Your colleagues in the classroom must feel like punching bags. We pay them so little to do so much and then want to put all the blame on them because our schools don't perform up to our standards.

Somehow we want to hold our schools to a higher standard of accountability than we are willing to place on ourselves. The fact is that our public schools mirror our society. Drugs, single-parent homes, a lack of respect for authority, permissiveness, the absence of civility—all impact our schools negatively. Yet we expect the teacher or the school board or the governor to solve our problems for us. We can't seem to bring ourselves to admit that the solutions must come from the home.

There will be days you will get so frustrated you will wonder why you became a teacher in the first place, but don't let that affect you. You have the unique opportunity to be a positive and lasting influence on young people. Don't lose your focus or forget why you are in the classroom. If you make a difference in just one life, all the irritations will have been worth it.

Every one of us can name a specific teacher that had an impact on our lives. Mine is Dr. Raymond Cook, a retired English Literature professor from Georgia State. He came into my life just as I was about to flunk out of college. (I never said I was as smart as you!) Being in Dr. Cook's classroom inspired me to stay in school and graduate. As you know, I have had a wonderful career, but I can't imagine what my life might have been like had I decided to quit school. That is the result that one teacher had on one student. I am not proud to say that it took me 43 years to tell him "thank you" but thank God, I finally did.

You may never have a student tell you what you have meant to him or her, and some of them may not even realize the effect you had, but that's okay because you will know in your heart that you made them better people. That is all that matters.

So it is now time to embark on this new and exciting journey with the applause of the whole family, particularly your old man. I wish you all the best. Woodland High School in Bartow County has landed a terrific biology teacher. And I have a terrific son.

Love, Dad

Dole's Solution to the "I" Problem

May 21, 2001

Look out, Bob Dole. Here comes Dick Yarbrough.

Bob Dole, former United States Senator, Republican presidential candidate, host of *Saturday Night Live* and spokesperson for Pepsi Cola and for Viagra, is widely known for referring to himself in the third person. After reading his mail this week, Dick Yarbrough thinks he should emulate Bob Dole.

Dick Yarbrough gets lots of reaction to his columns. He has upset blacks for saying that Jesse Jackson probably won't get his vote as Father of the Year. He was called a coward by whites, who disagreed with his stand on changing the state flag. One retired football coach (not Vince Dooley) didn't like Dick Yarbrough pointing out that Max Cleland has one of the most liberal voting records in the Senate and suggested an "eye-to-eye" meeting. (Only if Dick Yarbrough can wear a helmet and doesn't have to do pushups.)

Democrats are convinced that Dick Yarbrough is a right-wing reactionary because he said Bill Clinton had "the morals of a coon dog." Dick Yarbrough was more concerned about being sued for slander by coon dog owners. Republicans, on the other hand, think he is in Roy Barnes' pocket after he said the GOP representatives in the General Assembly are so inept at doing battle with the governor they "couldn't find their backside with both hands." Even BellSouth, the company for whom he toiled so long and enthusiastically, got upset with Dick Yarbrough because of his criticism of the Georgia Public Service Commission. He had wondered aloud how the PSC could successfully manage such complicated matters as natural gas deregulation with a chairman named Bubba. A BellSouth official who has a number of critical issues before the Commission promptly fired off a letter saying that Bubba is a perfectly fine name, thank you. Be assured that Dick Yarbrough now agrees. Bubba is a wonderful name.

But the letter responsible for this column came from a reader who complained about how many times the word "I" appears in

Dick Yarbrough's columns. It had to be obvious because the writer also said he puts the column in the "Don't Read" category. Dick Yarbrough was afraid to ask him how he knew that there were too many "I" words in his columns if he didn't read them. But it can happen. Georgia House Speaker Tom Murphy castigated Dick Yarbrough earlier this year when Dick Yarbrough said the Speaker was "toast" after having barely squeaked through his last election. Mr. Speaker began his letter by saying he never reads my—oops!—Dick Yarbrough's column, but he vehemently disagreed with the notion that he was on his Last Hurrah. Dick Yarbrough is perplexed, but evidently some folks can absorb his thoughts by osmosis. What makes that even more remarkable is that many people who carefully read Dick Yarbrough's writings each week tell him they don't have the foggiest idea what he is talking about. Even Dick Yarbrough is not always sure what he is saying, and he writes this stuff.

But Dick Yarbrough said, "If Bob Dole can avoid the 'I' word, so can Dick Yarbrough." Granted, we don't have much else in common—Bob Dole and you-know-who. Dick Yarbrough is not interested in getting into politics. It is more fun standing on the sidelines and sniping at those who do. Dick Yarbrough doesn't drink Pepsi because he is a Coca-Cola loyalist. Dick Yarbrough will never host *Saturday Night Live* because he has to be in bed by 10 P.M. Dick Yarbrough doesn't rule out a shot at being Viagra's spokesperson, but that is a subject for another day.

But like Bob Dole, Dick Yarbrough rises to the challenge. He was motivated by the reader to write a column not using the "I" word. He did. Dick Yarbrough hopes he is not asked to do that again. It is difficult to say what he wants to say if he can't use that other word occasionally. That is why he admires Bob Dole for being able to go through life always talking in the third person. He makes it look so easy. When Dick Yarbrough thinks about that, he just shakes his head in awe and says, "How Bob Dole is able to do that is beyond I."

Ethics Law
Loophole
Courts Disaster

We are fortunate in Georgia that we have managed to avoid some of the scandals and improprieties that have hit other state governments.

But watch out. We have the potential for a major disaster because of a loophole in our ethics law big enough to drive a road-grading machine and a contract full of high-tech goodies through. Georgia currently has one of the weakest ethics laws in the country. I know. I serve as a member of the State Ethics Commission. State law mainly confines our activities to monitoring disclosure forms submitted by elected officials and lobbyists. Left out of that law is any oversight of a group of people who call themselves contractors and consultants. However they describe themselves, they function much like lobbyists, actively competing for a piece of the $14 billion in the current state budget for themselves or their clients, only they don't have to tell anybody what they are doing. It's the law.

The backgrounds of these consultant/contractors are impressive. Some are wealthy businessmen. Some are former state legislators or congressmen. Some were chiefs of staff to governors. Some were elected to statewide office in another life. Some are former law partners to government influentials. Some manage statewide election campaigns for key officials. All have impeccable contacts inside state government and considerably more influence on how the state budget gets spent than many registered lobbyists. They don't have to register, according to the law, because they don't "influence legislation," i.e., lobby the Legislature. That is because they don't have to. They wheel and deal at the top of state government. Nobody knows who they see or what strings they pull for themselves and their clients.

A registered lobbyist takes a legislator to a ballgame or buys breakfast, and that has to be reported to the Ethics Commission. That is only fair because you have a right to know who is influencing the expenditures of your tax dollars. What isn't fair is that a contractor can provide a vacation home to an elected official and doesn't have to report it, or that contractors and consultants can quietly apply their considerable clout with state agencies for projects that can and often do compete with a registered lobbyist, who doesn't have the same access. One high-powered—and unregistered—consulting firm even brags on their Web pages about their "full blown lobbying initiative" for one of their clients.

There is blame enough to go around on why we allow this kind of good ol' boy network to exist without full public disclosure. The easiest target is, of course, the Legislature. As if the ethics laws aren't weak enough, there was a brief attempt by a group of legislators in the last session, led by House majority leader Larry Walker, of Perry, to weaken the laws even further. Happily, it didn't get very far, and if it rears its ugly head next year, I will decimate a forest for the newsprint to fight it.

The media deserves some of the blame. They know this stuff is going on but with the exception of Dale Russell, of Fox5 in Atlanta and veteran political reporter Bill Shipp, most have chosen to sit on their duffs and ignore the issue.

But we must share the blame, too. Politicians make decisions in only one of two ways: either through pressure applied or by an absence of pressure. In the case of strong ethics law, we have shown that we don't seem to care how the state spends our money. Our lawmakers equate that to a lack of pressure.

There is some good news. The Georgia Technology Authority is going to require contractor/consultants to register before the GTA's $600 million to $1 billion contract is let out for bids, and Republican Sonny Perdue, of Bonaire, introduced a bill to force these consultant-types to play by the same rules as registered lobbyists.

There is simply too much state government money available to many consultants who have too much influence, too much access and too little accountability. The state should not allow its business to be handled behind closed doors. Governor Roy Barnes prides himself on openness. He can do us all a favor by insisting that all the contractors and consultants and lobbyists seeking state contracts do their business in public.

That noted political philosopher, Groucho Marx, once said, "Politics is the art of looking for trouble, finding it, diagnosing it incorrectly and applying the wrong remedies."

He just described our ethics laws.

The Human
Touch in
Business

My friend, former colleague and fellow Bulldog, Carl Swearingen, senior vice president and secretary of BellSouth Corporation, is retiring. To the best of my knowledge, he is the last of a breed of managers raised up in the business by the legendary Jasper Dorsey, and BellSouth will be poorer for not having any more of Jasper's disciples around. For many years, Jasper Dorsey was vice president of Southern Bell's operations in Georgia when that office had all the responsibility for providing telephone service in the state. More importantly, he was the best manager and the best developer of people that I have ever known

I count myself extremely fortunate to have worked for Jasper, although I didn't think it was much, an honor at the time I was going through the fire. Jasper Dorsey was one tough man to please. No matter how well you did, he always thought you could do better. For young managers like Carl and me and the others who labored in his vineyard, there was scant margin for error. Those who couldn't take the pressure soon faded away. Those who could not only grew as managers but more importantly as human beings.

Carl Swearingen and I learned a lot from Jasper. We learned that before business, there was family and church. (A close fourth was the University of Georgia.) We learned that you were expected to put something back into the community, like your time and your talent. We learned that details are very important. Jasper said that if he couldn't trust his managers with the little things—like making sure not one misspelled word ever crossed his desk—he sure couldn't trust them with the big things. We learned that the customer always—always—came first. I often wonder what Jasper would do today if he had to tolerate the impersonal service that most all businesses give to customers. I know the reason they do it. Recordings don't require pay raises, benefits and don't need sick days. In truth, it is a cheaper way to run the business. But that wouldn't fly with Jasper. He would have figured out some way to have customers in Georgia deal with a live human being whenever they called the company, and he would have figured out a way to make it profitable. He was Home Depot before there was a Home Depot.

Carl and I also learned to appreciate the power of the external environment from him. He was the pro when it came to media relations and government relations and his methods would work today if PR people would simply apply them. Jasper said that in dealing with the media and politicians, there was room for only one ego and it wasn't ours. He would reluctantly accept media criticism of the company, only if he were convinced that you had given it your best shot in trying to explain the company's position on a given issue. But God help you if he saw something critical written or said about Southern Bell and you had not bothered to make your case. He would assume you didn't know the people in the media and he would quickly find someone who did. You didn't get a second chance.

Today we live in different times. Since I have been writing this column, I have given BellSouth a mild case of heartburn from time to time. Only one person from the company has made an effort to sit down with me and show me the errors of my ways. That was Carl Swearingen. Jasper Dorsey would have had somebody virtually living with me were he around today.

Perhaps I am being too critical of my alma mater. There are far bigger issues on BellSouth's plate—international expansion, share price, mergers and acquisitions—than in the simple days when I was coming along. Maybe Jasper Dorsey's style of management would be irrelevant in today's high-tech, fast-changing world. But somehow I don't think so. No matter how much business changes, it still boils down to good customer service. Jasper's mantra was "If it doesn't please the customer, it doesn't count." That sounds pretty up-to-date to me.

So to my friend, Carl Swearingen, I say congratulations and best wishes in retirement. You have had a great career at BellSouth. Jasper Dorsey would be pleased at how well you did but not surprised. He knew if you survived him, everything else would be a piece of cake.

Never-Blame-
Yourself
Society

Tobacco products—especially cigarettes—have all the redeeming qualities of a fence post. I smoked a cigarette once when I was at the University of Georgia. I was trying to be cool. I got such a bad case of heartburn that I never smoked another one. So much for being cool.

According to the Communicable Disease Center in Atlanta, cigarette smoking is responsible for 90 percent of lung cancers among men and 79 percent among women. People who smoke two or more packs of cigarettes a day have lung cancer mortality rates 12 to 25 times greater than nonsmokers. Smoking is responsible for 30 percent of all cancer deaths, as well as a lot of bad breath, stained teeth and smelly clothes.

Society has made smoking so politically incorrect that most smokers must feel strongly about their right to light up just to endure the angry glare of those of us who would prefer they lick an ashtray instead.

As repugnant as it is, however, smoking isn't against the law. As a matter of fact, it is perfectly legal. While we can limit where people smoke, we cannot deny their right to smoke.

That is why I question the recent jury decision in California that awarded $3 billion to Richard Boeken, a two-pack-a-day smoker. Mr. Boeken—a lifelong smoker—has lung and brain cancer but says he wasn't aware of the dangers of smoking until just a few years ago. Not aware of the dangers? Where has this guy been? On Mars? Maybe the smoke was so thick in his house he couldn't see the warning labels that have been on cigarette packages since 1965. Maybe he was too busy sucking nicotine to pay attention to all of the media reports on the dangers of smoking. Maybe the American Cancer Society doesn't have a branch office on Mars.

I have no sympathy for Philip Morris, which got nailed by the jury. The company makes a dangerous product and deserves a good kick in the pocketbook. Besides, cigarette manufacturers have a history of being less than forthright about the hazards of smoking. But Philip Morris didn't force Mr. Boeken to buy their product. He did of his own free will. And if the companies can be sued for making tobacco available for purchase, what about the tobacco farmers? It is a $150 million business in Georgia. Why don't we sue them for growing the stuff in the first place?

The answer is that too many people—almost 50 million in the U.S.—still want to smoke and chew and dip. And as long as they do, the nation will continue to allow tobacco products into the marketplace. Government will continue to pay subsidies to tobacco farmers who ought to do something responsible for a change, like grow kumquats. Lawyers will continue to get rich suing deep-pocketed tobacco companies. Anti-smoking groups will continue to rail about the dangers of tobacco. But tobacco products are going to be with us until you and I get fed up and exert enough pressure on Congress to ban the stinky stuff once and for all. Until then, people will be free to exercise their legal right to go eyeball-to-eyeball with cancer. It is the American way.

But I have a big problem with not taking responsibility for our actions. That also seems to be the American way these days. A guy smokes two packs of cigarettes a day for forty years, gets cancer and then says it isn't his fault. Philip Morris made him do it. Can't we ever say, "I made a mistake?" "I goofed?" "I'm wrong?" "My fault?" Evidently not. It has become a part of our culture to point the finger at somebody else for our sins. We drive gas-guzzling SUVs too fast and then blame the government for high gas prices. We drink too much, eat too much, fool around too much, and then wonder who is responsible for a decline in morality. We are afraid to tell our kids 'no' and then we chastise our education system for a lack of discipline. We cluck about all the inept politicians in Washington and less than half of us even bother to vote. There seems to be no end to our abilities to pass the buck for our shortcomings.

Mr. Boeken blames Philip Morris for giving him cancer. Maybe somebody should tell him to go look in a mirror. He might see the real culprit. Maybe we need to take an occasional peek ourselves.

Reflections
on Our Nation's
Birthday

In case you haven't noticed, this great nation of ours is having a birthday. She is 225 years old and doing just fine, thank you. She has survived foreign wars, civil wars and cold wars. Born in revolution and not given much of a chance to survive, the United States is today the freest, richest, most powerful and most compassionate country on earth. And the most envied.

You are no doubt aware that a lot of people overseas don't seem to like us. It is hard to pick up the paper or watch the evening news without seeing some jerkwater country demonstrating against a perceived ill perpetrated on them by the bad ol' United States. (Of course, they do still accept our money.) The media tend to view these demonstrations as momentous events, which they most certainly are not. For example, when a bunch of Swedes, who wouldn't recognize a 40-hour workweek if it was tattooed on their eyelids, booed President Bush on his recent trip there, the media damn near hyperventilated. I say, "So what?" Having Sweden not love us is akin to being ostracized by Elmer Fudd.

But it isn't the attitude of other countries that worries me. It's you and me. We take our democracy as a given. Sadly, we are losing the very people who are the best reminders of the price of freedom—the men and women of World War II. Never have there been braver people. One only needs to look at the cliffs of Normandy or the sunken memorials at Pearl Harbor to know that. These volunteer soldiers crushed two evil empires simultaneously and then the survivors came home and got on with their lives. We will never see their equal again.

Hopefully, our generation and those that follow can live in a more secure world, but don't count on it. Between our enemies and our apathy, there are no guarantees. We are all in bad need of a civics lesson. Recently, my 13-year-old grandson, Brian, was required to interview a public official as a step toward attaining the rank of First Class in his local Boy Scout troop. My friend, Rich

Golick, a member of the state legislature, kindly agreed to meet with Brian and talk to him about citizenship.

It was a conversation that should be required of every citizen in the United States (although I suspect Rep. Golick doesn't have the time to meet with all 280 million of us.) He reminded Brian of the extraordinary freedoms that we have in the United States—freedom of speech, freedom of the press, freedom of worship, due process—but he also emphasized the responsibilities that come with those freedoms—to pay our taxes, accept the call to jury service and, most important, to vote. We want our freedoms but aren't quite as enthusiastic about accepting our responsibilities. We forget how good we have it. We forget how high the tax rate is in other countries. We forget that many countries don't allow jury trials. We forget that in many countries, voting is a joke, if it occurs at all.

We have been blessed beyond anything our Founding Fathers could have imagined. Yet, if we aren't careful, we will do what no foreign power has been able to accomplish in over two centuries—bring about our downfall. Somebody or something has got to reunite us. Make us appreciate what we have. Make us proud to be Americans. A good start would be to get rid of the hyphen. It seems that every group in the country wants to be hyphenated. We want to be known as African-Americans, Asian-Americans, Mexican-Americans, Arab-Americans and so on. Poppycock! We are Americans, pure and simple. There is no reason not to be proud of our heritage but hyphens divide us, rather than unite us.

Being openly patriotic is politically incorrect these days. There is no shortage of critics both overseas and at home anxious to tell us what is wrong with us, but too few of us are willing to wave the flag and celebrate all that is right about us.

Frankly, I don't give a rat's backside about what the rest of the world thinks of us. I subscribe to Stephen Decatur's philosophy. It was this great naval war hero of 1812 who proclaimed, "To our country! In her intercourse with foreign nations, may she always be in the right; but our country, right or wrong."

I couldn't have said it better. Happy birthday, America.

Waging War Against the Squirrels

I don't know if word has reached the folks at the United Nations or the Geneva Convention or wherever they talk about these sorts of things, but my wife has declared war on squirrels. Total and unconditional, scorched-earth war. No suing for peace and that kind of stuff. We are talking major conflict here.

One of her first acts as Commander in Chief was to appoint me brigadier general. My orders are clear. Don't touch the remote control. Don't pick up a golf club. Don't worry about Alan Greenspan and interest rates. Just get rid of the squirrels and get rid of them now.

In my opinion, this unpleasantness could have been avoided had the squirrels used a little discretion. They are clearly the aggressors.

There is plenty of room in our backyard for all of God's creatures. Our policy has always been to "live and let live." Well, that is not totally true. The Commander in Chief doesn't include snakes in that policy. As a result, over the past couple of years I have killed two copperheads that made the mistake of trespassing into our yard. I also captured a king snake and managed to save its life by telling her that king snakes will kill and eat copperheads, which gave me strong personal motivation to see it live. King snakes also eat all kinds of other bad things—including asparagus. It almost cost me a marriage but she finally relented and allowed me to take the snake to my daughter's house out in the country, where it slithered off in search of a rodent or another snake or some asparagus.

But the squirrels wouldn't cooperate. All kinds of things are available on the ground for them to eat—nuts and such—but they prefer to eat out of our two birdfeeders. These aren't just birdfeeders; they are "squirrel-proof" birdfeeders. Obviously, the squirrels considered this discriminatory and an abridgment of their rights to feed whenever and wherever they want. Rather than bother the ACLU, which specializes in nut cases, the squirrels took matters into their own paws. They learned how to open the squirrel-proof birdfeeders, chase off the birds, climb inside, gorge themselves and then dump the remaining seeds on the ground for other squirrels. Hence, the declaration of war.

I am new at this brigadier general business, and there aren't many military experts left in Georgia who can help me since the Bush administration is closing down military bases faster than I can find them. I figured that the first thing I needed to do was arm to the teeth. So I bought a genuine Daisy Red Ryder BB gun, just like the one I had when I was a kid except this weapon has a trigger lock and a bunch of brochures with lawyer language about the dangers of BB guns. BB guns didn't have trigger locks when I was growing up, and my dad provided all the warnings I ever needed. I doubt I ever shot my Red Ryder without first enduring the "you can put your eye out with that thing" lecture.

So far, it hasn't been much of a war. The little critters can hear the door opening, and they scramble to safety before Red Ryder and I can get our collective act together. But if the squirrels spent as much time gathering information on their enemy as they do sneaking into the squirrel-proof birdfeeders, they could relax and enjoy the hostilities. Their spies might tell them that the brigadier general is old and addled and wears trifocals. Further intelligence would confirm that by the time I get the gun sight focused, I forget what I am shooting at.

In the meantime, I am neglecting my other duties, like overseeing the state legislature's plans to reapportion the Republicans into one congressional district in Alabama, working with Governor Roy Barnes on a new state flag design to see if we can make it any uglier than it already is, and advising Delta Air Lines on its plans to remove the aisles from all of their airplanes in order to add more seats. I really don't have time to make war on squirrels. The world needs me.

I just hope the king snake reads this and will come back home and take care of the squirrels for me. The Commander in Chief will never have to know.

I'll even throw in some asparagus free of charge.

Some Advice
for Beijing
Olympics

As you know by now, the demigods at the International Olympic Committee have awarded the 2008 Olympic Games to that bastion of democracy, Beijing, China. If you aren't familiar with the location, it is the home of Tiananmen Square where tanks run over people holding views that differ from the tank commanders' bosses. Lovely spot.

China's human rights record hasn't been—well—spotless. But the IOC is confident that will change once they get the government to stop roughing up members of the Falun Gong spiritual group and focus on the Games. After all, the Olympic poobahs held the 1936 Games in Germany, and we all know what a tremendous impact that had on world peace. Same with the Winter Games in Sarejevo in 1984.

But China does have some positives to offer. For one thing, they aren't real big on dissension. I am going to offer to send Atlanta newspaper columnist Colin Campbell and cartoonist Mick Luckovich to Beijing at my expense in hopes they would second-guess the organizing committee there as they did Atlanta so I can watch them neck deep in a rice paddy when they do. I would pay double if Izzy, ACOG's much-maligned mascot, were assigned to stand guard over them with an AK-47.

I doubt that China would welcome the involvement of Munson Steed, either. He is the genius that put Atlanta on the map with the renowned sidewalk vendors program that made television viewers around the world think they had tuned into a third-world flea market, not a world-class sporting event.

When I was a member of the 1996 Centennial Games staff, I thought we would have to extend the Olympics for six months in order to accommodate all of the special interest groups that fervently sought their 15 minutes of fame in the worldwide spotlight. You name 'em, we had 'em: Jesse Jackson (naturally), gays, feminists, Hispanics, pro-state flag supporters, anti-state flag supporters, environmentalists, animal rights activists, the list goes on and on. The protesters varied but not their tactics—trying to hold

Olympic planners hostage by demonstrations, media manipulation, intimidation, and any other means necessary to get a piece of the action or face time on television.

Somehow I don't believe these groups are going to have much luck in China, unless they desire some quality time with the Falun Gong folks in the local pokey. I don't think gays will threaten to throw buckets of water on the Olympic flame during the torch relay as they claimed they would in 1996 in order to elicit sympathy to their plight. I doubt the labor unions will try to close down Olympic construction in Beijing. Tree huggers will have about as much luck lassoing snail darters as influencing Chinese environmental policies. And don't expect any conversation about changing the Chinese flag. Even Roy Barnes wouldn't touch that one.

There will be several exciting new events in the Beijing Games. Pin the Tail on the Dissident will feature blindfolded contestants jabbing acupuncture needles in the backside of any citizen dumb enough to bad-mouth the government between now and 2008. Chinese Checkers will highlight the ability of border guards to make sure nobody leaves the country in order to bad-mouth the government between now and 2008. The Peking Duck competition will be limited to Chinese officials who will attempt to evade questions about China's record on human rights, pollution, jailing of journalists, concentration camps and a host of other topics the locals don't seem inclined to ask. I don't know about you but I can't wait.

Lost in the hubbub about Beijing's selection is that the International Olympic Committee has a new president. Dr. Jacques Rogge, a Belgian orthopedic surgeon, will replace his Imperial Majesty Juan Antonio Samaranch, who presided over the IOC for 21 years and was best known for declaring every Olympics as the "Best Games Ever," except for the Atlanta Games which he called, "The Games with the Most Interesting Sidewalk Vendors Program." Whether Dr. Rogge continues this tradition through the Salt Lake Winter Games ("The Best Games Ever in Utah") and the 2004 Athens Games ("The Best Games Ever in Athens with the Exception of the 1968 Game When the Dawgs Kicked Tech's Butts, 47-8"), remains to be seen.

Dr. Rogge hasn't consulted me on what to do, but if he asks, I would suggest waiting until after 2008 to change that policy. Otherwise, he may find himself in Tiananmen Square nose-to-nose with a cranky tank driver.

Dear Baby: Words of Welcome

Dear Kathleen Devere Worthley,

Welcome to the world. We are glad you have arrived. I thought your mama and daddy had outdone themselves when they created corn-fried shrimp at the exquisite little Georgia Sea Grill on St. Simons Island, but you are without question their greatest creation.

Your presence has been much anticipated. Things haven't been going too well on the planet. I'm afraid those of us in charge have done a poor job of minding the store. We seem to have accumulated more than an ample number of self-absorbed and ill-humored individuals. What we desperately need are a few kind and gentle and loving souls. That is why we applaud your appearance. We need you.

I suspect your top priorities right now are food and sleep, and the last thing you want is advice from some guy you haven't even met. But as people who regularly read this space will tell you, I always have advice to offer, whether anybody wants it or not, so please bear with me.

First off, I urge you to try and make the world better than you found it. Given the current state of affairs, it shouldn't be hard to do. You aren't going to have much competition for the job. Most of us are too caught up in our own self-concerns to care about anything or anybody else. Making the world better really isn't as daunting as it sounds. You don't have to find a cure for cancer or save the Brazilian rain forest or write The World's Great Novel, although any such activity would be welcomed. Just do something nice for somebody every day of your life. Nothing big. Usually a smile or a "thank you" will suffice and, believe it or not, these simple gestures can make the world better because they might just inspire other people to do the same.

Try as hard as you can to not be judgmental of people. We all have some good, although finding it may be hard at times.

Be passionate and don't be afraid to dream big dreams. Too many people sleepwalk through life, simply occupying space and time. Find something that stirs you and do it to the very best of your abilities. It may be a talent—art or music or sports or science or some cause such as the environment or literacy or helping people less fortunate than you. What excites you isn't as important as the fact that you care deeply about something.

Be patriotic. I hope you get a lump in your throat every time you hear "The Star-Spangled Banner" like I do. You live in the greatest country on earth, but don't take your freedoms for granted. Some very brave people sacrificed their lives to ensure that you and I wouldn't have to sacrifice ours. Don't be ashamed to love your country. Remind people who are so quick to point out our faults that they are lucky to live in a land where they can complain. In a lot of other countries, they would be wielding a pickax in a salt mine. And please vote every time you have the opportunity. Casting a ballot is the most serious obligation you will ever have as an American citizen.

Enjoy life. Watch the sun rise over the marshes at St. Simons and set in the mountains of Rabun County and realize how small we really are in the grand scale of the universe. Don't take things too seriously. Enough of us already do that. We spend so much time grinding over what happened to us yesterday or worrying about what may happen tomorrow, but yesterday and tomorrow are the two things we can't control. Live in this day and don't waste a minute of it. Rejoice in God's miracles like rain showers, red roses, vanilla ice cream, lightning bugs and Ray Charles singing "Georgia on My Mind." Lordy, can that man sing!

I know I have given you a lot to mull over in your first few days here, Kate, but you have plenty of time and I'm sure you'll come up with some ideas of your own. You come from good stock, and I am confident that you are going to make a positive difference in this world. I look forward to watching you grow and hope that one day we can continue this conversation over a plate of corn-fried shrimp. It will be my pleasure.

Redistricting:
Politics at
Its Worst
August 13, 2001

Allow me to offer a slightly different perspective on the redistricting session currently underway at the state capitol. The whole thing is about as meaningful as bifocals on a boar hog. It is a private party for politicians, special interest groups and assorted political junkies. No voters need apply.

I generally defend politicians because the vast majority are first-rate people trying to do a good job. They put up with a lot of unnecessary abuse and stereotyping they don't deserve. But redistricting isn't their finest hour. Rather, it is Exhibit A in why politicians have an image worse than almost anybody except column writers.

Our political leaders are supposed to be redrawing the state map to ensure that our congressional districts and legislative districts have about the same number of people in them. This is done every decade and is especially significant this time around because we have a lot more people than we did in 1990. Many of our new residents are Yankees who moved to Georgia because they thought they were escaping other Yankees, only to find out that a bunch of them were already here. Most chose not to move back when they remembered that the summer season in the Northeast runs from August 5–12, so we are obliged to count them.

You would think it would be easy—even for politicians—to take the number of people in the state and divide them up into similar sized districts. They could be home by midweek, even allowing for the fact that because of our growth, we have to find a place for two new congressional districts. (Currently, our state has ten members of Congress, plus Cynthia McKinney, who doubles as Special Ambassador to Outer Space, which is where her head is most of the time.)

But redistricting isn't about redistricting. It is about power politics. It is the time when those in power reward their friends and punish their enemies. An example: You have a representative from your district who has done a good job for you, who has generally voted the way you expected, and has given you good constituent service. But your elected official may have had the temerity to vote against Roy Barnes a time or two, or maybe he or she didn't fawn hard enough over House Speaker Tom Murphy or maybe your representative is a (gasp!) Republican. Too bad. It makes no difference how well they have represented you. Redistricting will assign them to the political trash heap.

The fact that redistricting is under the firm control of Democrats is not good news for the Republicans. Like you and me, they will be standing on the outside looking in as special interest groups crawl under the covers with the Democratic leadership and draw up districts that will probably have most Republicans bunched together somewhere out in Wyoming. By all rights, Georgia should have a strong, viable Republican Party, but they can't seem to get their act together. Many of them think that defending the long-dead state flag is a cutting-edge issue that will catapult them to power in 2002. I suspect that Ralph Reed, chairman of the state Republican Party, will one day be able to convince his members that it isn't the nineteenth century anymore, but it won't be in time to stop the bleeding from this redistricting session.

This may be the Democrats' last opportunity to maintain their stranglehold on state politics and they will take full advantage of the opportunity to weaken Republicans everywhere they can—except for the eight GOP congressmen who they don't want running against their stealth senator, Max Cleland. They will be sure to take special care of their black members, even at the expense of other members of their own party. And a number of good, hard-working and dedicated legislators will be shown the door. Speaking of the door, it belongs to the governor and it will be closed during most of the meaningful discussions on redistricting.

When the politicians finally get through this meaningless exercise, they will no doubt heap praise on themselves for their heroic efforts on our behalf, accompanied by eye-glazing analysis from political pundits on just what it all means. As for you and me, we will be expected to tamely accept the decisions of a group of wheeling and dealing insiders bent on protecting their turf. After all, we are only voters.

It is politics at its worst and it stinks.

Ready for Battle
Against the
PC Police

Maybe it is my age or the dog days of summer or maybe I am just having a bad hair day, but I am fed up with political correctness. The majority of people in this country have been intimidated and paralyzed to the point that they are afraid to say anything lest some minority group be offended. This phenomenon has occurred because special interest groups have learned how to manipulate the media, which, in turn, manipulate the politicians, leaving the rest of us with no voice. We are fair game for criticism but if we in turn dare to criticize, we are deemed homophobic, racist, sexist, bigoted or worse. The PC police are holding us hostage, and I for one am tired of it.

For example, Patrick Leahy, senior senator from the pipsqueak state of Vermont, doesn't swear in people with the traditional "So help me God" anymore. Might offend somebody. Wonder if he ever thought that it might offend God? Maybe Senator Goofy will have a chance to find out firsthand one day.

Law-breaking foreigners who sneak into our country are no longer "illegal aliens." They are now referred to as "undocumented immigrants."

The city of Atlanta is hyperventilating over the possibility of hosting the Gay Games in 2006, despite the fact that the city badly bungled the 1996 Centennial Olympic Games—or should we refer to them as the Heterosexual Games? The city's politicians and business leaders spent most of their time five years ago trying to make a buck off the Games, and the local media was too worried about the woebegone Olympic mascot, Izzy, to focus on making a dysfunctional city work. Hurling brickbats at the organizing committee became an Olympic sport. As a result, Atlanta looked to the world like a cheap flea market. But the Gay Games will have no problems with the politicians, the business community or the media. Nobody has the guts to dare criticize them as they did us. Gays win the gold medal when it comes to intimidating people who disagree with them.

Jesse Jackson has an affair with a staff member and produces a baby out of wedlock. It barely causes a ripple in the media. Jackson criticizes Anheuser-Busch for something or other and his son suddenly ends up with a lucrative beer distributorship. Questions are raised about the coincidence of that chain of events and Jackson says such speculation is—tah dah—racist. Everybody quickly goes mute. Now let's suppose that Charlton Heston, part-time Moses and full-time white guy who serves as president of the National Rifle Association, had done what Jackson did and ended up with one illegitimate baby and a few hundred beer trucks for his kids. There aren't enough trees in the forest to supply the newsprint required for the huffing and puffing that the press would do. And we would likely deplete the ozone layer with the hair spray needed for all the hyperventilating television commentators. Double standard? You bet your sweet backside there is a double standard.

Before we go off and slash our politically incorrect wrists, the good guys just might win one for a change. The Boy Scouts of America decided some time ago that they don't want gays as scout leaders. I know some gays I think would make pretty good scout leaders, but that's not the point. The point is that the Boy Scouts have the right to decide who leads their organization and who doesn't. This claim for freedom and independence, of course, didn't sit well with gay rights groups, which made their usual snarling threats. But they have hit a brick wall on this issue. Why? The Boy Scouts are a great source of pride to most Americans who have suddenly found their voice and have come roaring to the Scouts' defense. The bullies in the gay community realize this and have temporarily backed off, along with the media and the pandering politicians. But they will be back. They aren't used to losing, which raises a question: If the gays can have their own Olympic Games and bars and tours and choruses and marriages, why don't they start their own gay scout troop and leave the rest of us alone?

I admit that living in this society can be pretty discouraging for people who consider themselves middle of the road. Maybe you have given up and are resigned to letting the inmates run the asylum. Not me. I'm ready to fight on. Just call me the last angry man or, to be politically correct, the last complacency-challenged individual.

Return of the
Over-the-Hill
Gang

Just when I thought there was nothing left to look forward to but a rocking chair and Metamucil, doggone if a couple of old guys don't pull off a major coup. The Coca-Cola Company has announced that they are bringing back 65-year-old Brian Dyson as their chief operating officer. Hurrah! Then beleaguered General Motors hires 69-year-old car designer extraordinaire Bob Lutz to put some pizzazz in their fuddy-duddy line of automobiles. Double hurrah!

Take that, you Chardonnay-sipping hard bodies! You've had your day. Now the old folks are making a comeback. Pretty soon, when you step into an elevator you will hear nothing but Mantovani music. (Who is Mantovani? Look him up between trips to the sushi bar.) All you rappers be prepared for less Gangsta Boo and Little Phat J and more Nat King Cole and Ella Fitzgerald. I can't wait to hear your car windows rattle with Glenn Miller's "Sunrise Serenade." And from now on, the operative words are "Yes ma'am" and "Yes sir" and anybody saying, "Have a nice day" or "Yo" is going to be sent to North Dakota with no chance of parole. Life is good!

I had about decided that we old folks were the Forgotten Generation. I have more free time and more expendable income than at any time in my life but nobody wants my business. I am not in the right demographic target market. That is another way of saying I shave every day, which makes me too old for most advertisers. Television advertising is created by a bunch of kids barely out of puberty. They think that their peers are the only ones buying anything except Viagra pills and that the best way to reach them is to create commercials with screaming announcers and music that sounds like a Caterpillar tractor engine. Even the New York Stock Exchange, of all places, is running a television commercial that is hard to distinguish from an album of Puff Daddy's One and Only Hit. (As if kids with braces and acne are suddenly going to quit buying music videos and start buying stock.) That is about to change, boys and girls.

When Mr. Dyson arrives at Coca-Cola, I hope he will make his first order of business getting Coke out of aluminum cans and back in the familiar old green bottles where it belongs. And while he is at it, I wish he would put on the bottom of the drinks again the towns where the Coca-Cola was bottled. It used to be great fun to buy a Coke and see where it was originally bottled and argue over whose soft drink was from the longest distance away. Obviously, Dyson will have to make an exception for the state of Alabama and put "Open Other End" on the bottles over there; otherwise, they'll never figure it out.

Over at General Motors, Bob Lutz is expected to work the magic that made him a hero at Chrysler. It was Lutz who designed the PT Cruiser, the hottest vehicle on the road these days and a must-have for all the yuppies or Gen-Xers, or whatever they call themselves. What they don't know is that the PT Cruiser looks exactly like my Uncle Arthur's 1938 Oldsmobile on which I learned to shift gears. I predict that Lutz will get GM out of their doldrums with an exciting new model based on the 1950 Studebaker. Then, hopefully, the In Crowd will fall all over themselves selling their gas-guzzling SUVs in order to own this latest trendsetter, while we old geezers laugh our heads off.

If we can get more folks like Dyson and Lutz into positions of power, you are going to see a lot of changes for the better. There will be more family programming on television and less of those stupid "reality" shows. There will be more neighbors talking over the backyard fence and less e-mail. More kids playing Fox and Hounds. Fewer playing video games. More smiles. Fewer pagers. More service representatives. Less "Punch 1 if you have a problem." More Red Skelton. Less Dennis Miller. More worship. Less selfishness. More love of country. Less emphasis on hyphenating our heritage.

Maybe having a couple of old guys suddenly get big jobs in two of our largest corporations isn't a groundswell, but it is a good start. If nothing more is accomplished than getting Cokes back in those little green bottles and gas-guzzling SUVs off the road, the changes will have been worth it.

A New
Perspective
... Just in Time

I love my alma mater, the University of Georgia, but several issues have arisen recently that have bothered me and I felt like I couldn't get anybody's attention, despite the time and dollars I have given over the years. "Not to worry," a UGA official assured me. "We'll sit down and talk them over. We want you to be happy." What a nice coincidence. I wanted to be happy, too. But, alas, happy turned into big-time unhappy in a hurry. On the day of our meeting, my designated hand-holder never showed. He had to confer with a heavy hitter politician and waited until an hour and a half after our scheduled appointment to so inform me. Now the institution had a bigger problem on its hands—an unhappy former president of the national alumni association who also happens to write columns for a living. So much for happy. But the next day, I attended a memorial for John Yauger and the whole issue became moot.

Dr. John Yauger was a warm and wonderful person who had a host of debilitating illnesses but never let them destroy his spirit. He was a retired physician, a member of my church and an avid reader of my musings. Every Sunday, I could count on him to give me a forthright evaluation of what I had said the previous week and some equally forthright suggestions on what to say next week.

What struck me about his memorial service was that there was little said about his professional accomplishments, significant though they were. Dr. Yauger had played a major role in getting citizens in metro Atlanta immunized against polio with the Sabin polio vaccine in the mid-1960s. But as impressive as his career had been, it was his marvelous sense of humor, his love for people, and his devotion to his family that the speakers kept emphasizing. I looked at the gathered businessmen who had been members of his Boy Scout troop and who had applied his principles to their successful careers and thought that if we are put on earth to make a difference, John Yauger had succeeded with room to spare.

Dr. Yauger did a lot of big, important things in his career, but it was the seemingly small things that had everyone smiling and nodding and reflecting on this unique man's life. It was like a wake-up call. After the service, I realized that my disagreements with the University of Georgia weren't nearly as important as they had been when I arrived. What is important is that two of my grandsons have a new dog of undetermined pedigree named Sheila—have you ever heard of a dog named Sheila?—and are excited beyond words.

Cooling my heels for a no-show didn't seem such a big deal any more, either. What is a big deal is that my other two grandsons are making all A's at school. One is running track; the other is playing basketball and beating my brains out when we play Horse. (Don't tell him but I am delighted.)

I thought about the hullabaloo over the redistricting silliness at the State Capitol. Today, it seems totally irrelevant. What is relevant is having a family that loves a husband and father who too often placed his career concerns ahead of their concerns. I need to tell my son-in-law and daughter-in-law how much I care about them, too. They have been a part of the family for 17 years and I am grateful my kids were smart enough to marry them. I still wake up in a cold sweat thinking about who they could have married.

I am through fretting about the University of Georgia. They can handle their problems without me, which will be a great relief to us both. I have more pressing issues to deal with right now. As patriarch of the Yarbrough clan, I must officially welcome Shelia into the family before she can change her mind. Hound dogs are very discerning, you know. Once that is done, I need to challenge a certain grandson to one more game of Horse, knowing I have no chance of winning but relishing the competition.

Whether, like John Yauger, I leave this the world better off for my having been here depends on how I define what is important and what isn't. Loving families and hound dogs are. Missed appointments are not.

It is called perspective and I found mine just in time.

Where Do We Draw the Line?

September 17, 2001

Where do we draw the line?

How do we balance the rights of American people to exercise their extraordinary freedoms against the intent of people in the world —and in our own country—who choose to make their political statements not through a free press, but with cowardly acts of terrorism against innocent people?

The recent and unimaginable acts of terrorism are another tragic reminder that something has to change. We can't remain a free country and continue to endure the atrocities that have been committed against us. We must either curtail our freedoms to go where we want and say what we want and do what we want, or we must find an effective way to deal with the problem.

I speak from experience. I was with the Atlanta Committee for the Olympic Games, and the subject of terrorism was with us every day. I happened to be at the White House on the day of the bombing in Oklahoma City. The first thought that came to everybody's mind was—*Arab terrorists*. Little did anyone know at the time that it was Americans attacking Americans.

On an early Saturday morning at the midpoint of the 1996 Atlanta Olympic Games, I was awakened to be told that a bomb had gone off in Centennial Olympic Park, a place where thousands gathered every night in a wonderful celebration of goodwill among people from throughout the world. Despite the criticism the Olympics get—much of it deserved—the concept is sound. The Games are about peaceful competition—a substitute for war and this idea worked wonderfully until someone had to make a statement and decided to make it with a bomb. The perpetrator has never been caught, but the chances are excellent that he or she was an American.

I remembered a high-level security briefing with the FBI before the Games in which they told us how hard it is to prevent terrorism in a country that has the freedom of movement that we have. I won't describe the scenarios they gave us for the kinds of bad things that could happen because I don't think they would want me to, but suffice it to say, we are vulnerable. Not because our government doesn't take terrorism seriously, because it does. Rather, our way of life doesn't make it easy to catch all the nut cases, both here and abroad, who have an ax to grind.

Something has to be done. I don't want my grandchildren to have to grow up afraid for their lives. I don't want a bunch of cowards to continue to make their statements with the lives of innocent Americans. I don't want to endure another week like this one.

I have had the opportunity to see terrorism up close, and it is frightening. It is the act of cowards. The worst thing we can do is throw up our hands in desperation. That is exactly what terrorists want us to do. They want us to lose our will and our spirit. No chance.

The very first decision that Billy Payne and his staff made after the Olympic Park bombing was to declare that the Games would continue. It was a risky decision because at that point we didn't know what else might happen, but we did know that we would not be held captive by a sick mind. It was the right decision. It was almost as if the public wanted to make their own statement and they did. Huge crowds assembled for the competitions that day. We had a full contingent of volunteers. We sold more tickets that day for the next day's competition than we had done on any day previously. If the terrorist was trying to bring down the Games, he failed miserably.

I have a feeling we will react the same way to this unprecedented attack on our citizens. We won't be intimidated and we will severely punish the people who are responsible.

But what about the future? Are we willing to give up some of our freedoms in order to make it harder for foreign and domestic terrorists to commit their acts of violence and satisfy some grudge— real or perceived? Can we live as freely and openly as we have and not be subjected to random terrorism? Can we balance freedom and security?

Where do we draw the line?

This Is
Pearl Harbor
Times Two

September 24, 2001

Some random thoughts as I try to comprehend the incomprehensible:

The terrorist attack was extremely well-planned and executed with deadly precision, but the planners made a fatal mistake: overkill. Had they thought about it, they would have exploded a few car bombs from time to time to let us know they were there and rattled our nerves as they have done for years. This action was over the top. Never, ever underestimate the enemy. The terrorists did and they will pay a heavy price. We are mad as hell.

Please spare me the rhetoric that bombing terrorists and the countries who support terrorism makes us just like "them." These people don't understand rule of law. They only understand force. This is Pearl Harbor times two, folks. Our country has many wonderful assets but our naiveté is not one of them.

We don't pay much money to police and firefighters and military, but they are indispensable because they are willing to give their lives for us. The people we pay the most money to—athletes and actors—are totally irrelevant. They exist only to amuse us and to distract us, nothing more.

If the attendance at my church is any indication, a lot of people have found God since the attack. It wasn't hard to do. God hadn't been missing. We think we are invincible until we get scared and see how small and helpless we really are. It reminds me of my favorite piece of graffiti, supposedly seen on a prison wall: "God is dead—Friedrich Neitzche." And just below that, another line: "Friedrich Neitzche is dead—God."

Representative Barbara Lee of—where else?—California, was the single vote in Congress against retaliation. She said she wasn't convinced that military action would prevent further acts of international terrorism against the United States, but she didn't seem to have any ideas about what would. Lee represents that hotbed of good old-fashioned American virtue, Berkeley. They deserve each other.

Looking through my files, I came across a clipping from the *Atlanta Journal-Constitution* dated July 7, 2001, in which cartoonist Mick Luckovich explained why he draws George W. Bush like a small child with big ears: "Most caricaturists start out drawing presidents normal-sized, but as they make mistakes and suffer under the weight of the presidency, they're drawn smaller and smaller. W is the exception. He started out the presidency seeming not quite up to it, so I began drawing him tiny right off the bat. If he doesn't start to grow in office, readers of my cartoons are going to have to use a magnifying glass to see him." I was struck at the time that a guy who gets paid hard currency to draw pictures for a living was an expert on the American presidency. Now I hope he will draw a picture of himself with his foot in his mouth. I will supply the magnifying glass.

The only people who seem unaffected by current events are the Yuppie Boomers driving their gas-guzzling SUVs like maniacs on the freeway and tailgating anybody doing less than 80 mph. I guess they can't be bothered.

My column a few weeks ago about being held hostage by the PC police drew a lot of response. The vast majority of writers agreed that mainstream America had lost its voice to small, vocal, special interest groups and wondered if we would ever get it back. Lo and behold, the terrorists did it for us. Patriotism is back in vogue. National pride flourishes. We are unhyphenated Americans. But be prepared. The naysayers will return. Having people unified and feeling good about themselves is the worst thing that could happen to these mean-spirited, self-absorbed jerks. They couldn't survive if they didn't constantly remind us of our deficiencies.

I handled most of the events of the past week with a stiff upper lip, but when I saw members of Congress standing on the front steps of the United States Capitol singing "God Bless America," I lost it. It was a moment I will never forget. God bless them for doing it. It was great to watch our political leaders put their party politics behind them and place their nation's welfare first. They meant it and we needed it. When—and if—things return to normal and they restart their petty squabbles, remember they have their outstanding moments, too.

Finally, never again forget that each day is precious and never again take one for granted. God bless America.

Struggling
Back to
Normalcy

President Bush has urged us all to try and get our lives back to normal after our national nightmare. I couldn't agree more. Being the patriotic American that I am, I decided to do my part, so I promptly lost my briefcase.

I also forgot to turn off the lights when I left the room—any room. I found myself in the den looking for something, but I couldn't remember what I was looking for. I swung at a golf ball that I intended to hit 200 yards and rolled it about six feet. I dropped jelly on my shirt (dark jelly, light shirt). I got lost but refused to stop and ask directions. I wrote a column and wasn't sure whether to put commas inside the quotation marks or outside. I drank out of the milk bottle.

Mr. President, I declare myself back to normal.

I am not alone. My housemate and her friends have resumed their long-standing tradition of driving all over Hell's Half Acre to save fifty cents on a doodad that nobody needed in the first place. I long ago gave up trying to explain the concept of cost-benefit analysis to her—that the gas for the trip costs more than what they save on the unneeded doodad. I was wasting my breath. For her and her shopaholic pals, buying unneeded doodads is perfectly normal behavior.

Since you probably have been preoccupied watching Hillary Clinton suck her thumb and roll her eyes because George Bush seems to be putting consecutive sentences together and actually running the country, I am glad to report to you than normal seems to be breaking out all over the nation.

For example, Georgia Tech supporters are once again trying to explain to us plebeians why the graduation rate for their student-athletes falls slightly short of a school of fish.

Motorists are once again weaving in and out of traffic without the use of the little stick on their steering wheel. ("What's that thing? A turn signal? Whatever does it do?")

On the redistricting front, the Georgia Legislature continues to make us swell with pride at their bipartisan and selfless efforts to ensure that all Democrats be guaranteed lifetime employment and thus avoid the possibility of having to find real jobs.

Governor Roy Barnes has signed a bill that makes it illegal for anyone to run against him. It passed unanimously because Republicans weren't allowed to vote. In Georgia, that's normal.

The television networks are back to their regularly scheduled programs, which means running commercials continuously so that we don't have to look at Sam Donaldson and his awful toupee.

The AOL/Ted Turner/Looney Tunes/Time-Warner/Atlanta Braves have discovered it is September and that they are still in the pennant race. That is not normal. The players have called a team meeting to rectify the situation, lest they have to face the frightening prospects of post-season play.

Pat Robertson and Jerry Falwell have declared that the bombings occurred because God got mad at us. God has declared that Pat Robertson and Jerry Falwell don't have the foggiest idea of what He is thinking because He hasn't told them anything and doesn't plan to and for you not to listen to them. God recommends that you listen to Billy Graham instead. He's for real.

The Georgia Public Service Commission has announced that their offices this winter will be heated with wood. The PSC denied that the cost of natural gas had anything to do with their decision. They say they like the ambience of a crackling fire.

Georgia Natural Gas has announced that it has bought all the forests in the United States and will petition the Georgia PSC to allow them to deregulate the cost of the wood. They say such a move would greatly benefit Georgia consumers.

I am pleased to share this progress report with you as our nation continues to heal and things slowly return to normal. In these times, we can use all the normal we can get. As for me, I am going to continue to drink milk out of the bottle, leave the lights on, love my family and share this space with you. I will even accept the fact that unneeded doodads are and forever will be a part of my life.

Normal feels good.

They're baaaaaack!

The naysayers are beginning to find their voice again. It was only a matter of time. After enduring what must have been an agonizing several weeks of flag waving, patriotism and general good feeling in this country, the anti-American crowd is desperate to make us understand that a bunch of nut cases flying airplanes into tall buildings and killing innocent people is somehow our fault. Only in America!

The height—or depth—of USA-bashing came from Bill Maher of ABC's *Politically Incorrect*. From the safety of his studio in Los Angeles, some 3000 miles from Ground Zero in New York, he described the United States as "cowards" and the terrorists as "courageous." He later clarified his comments by saying our soldiers weren't cowards, just our government. Gosh, I'm glad he cleared that up. I feel better already! If reincarnation really happens, I hope this self-important snob comes back as a bug so I can have the pleasure of squashing him.

Frankly, I am kind of glad the naysayers are making a comeback because they are proving a point they would just as soon not make. This nation they think has so much wrong with it protects their right to trash it. Ironic, isn't it? Many countries would cut off the protesters' noses and feed them to the pigs. We choose to hold our noses and listen.

If naiveté were anthrax, we would all be dead by now. The naysayers need to leave their dream world more often because they show an abysmal amount of ignorance about the world. Terrorists are genuinely bad people who want to destroy us. They only understand brute force. They will be back to blow up more buildings or poison our water supply or spread God knows what kind of disease on loyalists and dissenters alike. We have no choice but to root them out and be rid of them. Although some people can't accept the notion, now and then the majority knows what is best for the country. In this case, the majority is tired of living under a constant terroristic threat. We are demanding that our government stop it once and for all.

I would respectfully suggest the naysayers quit worrying about face time on CNN and go down to Camden County or up to Union County or over to Madison County or into Monroe County and make their case with Middle America. Tell the rest of us face-to-face what is wrong with us and with our country. Convince us the United States is the only country that has ever committed a wrong in pursuit of its policies. Tell us about all the other countries that have something akin to our Peace Corps. List the countries that have a culture of citizens volunteering like the United States. Give us the names of other nations that work harder at equality for all of their citizens. Yes, we fall short but at least we keep trying. Give us your suggestions on what you would do to stop terrorism in the United States but be willing to have your opinions questioned because I guarantee you, there will be questions.

You are going to be asked about your insistence that innocent people not be killed. That doesn't resonate real well right now with us, because you haven't talked much about the innocent people we lost. War is not neat and war is not pretty. In fact, to quote a subject matter expert, William Tecumseh Sherman, war is hell. But if we wanted to deliberately kill innocent people, we would do like the terrorists and wipe out a bunch of them. Instead, we will do as General Norman Schwarzkopf said we did in the Gulf War; we will put our own soldiers at risk to avoid taking innocent lives. Be sure and tell us all the other countries that make that kind of effort.

So, keep it up, naysayers, because your babbling reminds us all of just how odious free speech can be at times and that only great democracies allow your kind of dissent when we need unity. Our tolerance is one of the qualities that make us unique. And we will go to war to preserve your right to try and make us feel bad about ourselves and to make cowards seem courageous. Only in America!

More Faith
in Government
Than Media

Conrad Fink is a professor at the Grady College of Journalism at the University of Georgia and a distinguished journalist. Fink has had an illustrious career as a reporter, foreign correspondent and vice president of Associated Press. As one who puts my time and tithes into the Grady College, I'm glad he is there, but I have a serious difference of opinion with him on the government's conduct in the war on terrorism.

In a recent column in the Athens *Banner-Herald*, Fink charged that the government is not sharing enough information with the news media on its plans to flush out the terrorists in Afghanistan and that it is wrong for the American people to agree with that decision.

In fact, Fink is wrong.

Fink cites his experiences in the Vietnam War, which he covered extensively for AP, as an example of how government tried to mislead the American public through evasion, distortion and outright lies. In the intervening years since Vietnam, we have learned not to trust our government with the childlike faith we once did, but we don't trust the media either, Professor.

To compare Vietnam to the current war against terrorism is to compare butter to butterflies. As unfortunate and divisive and traumatic as Vietnam was, our very existence was not at stake then. Now it is. Fink need look only at the students at the Grady College. The morning after the terrorist attacks, professors were ready to discuss the media coverage of the events of September 11. The students were more interested in knowing whether or not they were going to have a future. So much for the ol' Ivory Tower.

At the same time that Fink was lamenting how the government is feeding reporters sparse news "in the name of patriotism," a nitwit named Loren Jenkins, who is senior foreign editor of National Public Radio, was quoted in the *Chicago Tribune* as saying he would report the whereabouts of U.S. Special Forces on secret mission if he could because he doesn't feel any duty to "help out the government." His job, he says, is to "smoke 'em out." I assume that if our soldiers were killed and our national security compromised as a result of his irresponsible reporting, that would be okay with this modern-day Ernie Pyle. Excuse me, Professor Fink, but that kind of arrogant, almost treasonous attitude doesn't make me real anxious that your colleagues know much more than that Afghanistan is somewhere east of Mobile, Alabama. I'll take my chances with George Bush and Colin Powell, thank you.

As for the media, it has a growing credibility problem with the American people that needs to be addressed sooner rather than later. Public support is eroding as we speak. The First Amendment Center at Vanderbilt University in its 2001 survey reports that while 82 percent of those polled say that the media should keep the government in check, 71 percent also say that the government should keep the media in check. In another study by the Center in 1999, over half of all Americans said the media has too much freedom, a figure that is up dramatically from just two years earlier. Those numbers are disturbing and should serve as a wake-up to call to journalists and to those who teach them.

We are in a fight for our survival. The United States has an enemy that wants to eradicate us, pure and simple. We have told our government in no uncertain terms that we want the terrorists found and their hides permanently fried. Use whatever means it takes. We aren't choosy. Just get it done. If the media can help, fine. If not, then they need to stay the hell out of the way. This is a whole new world, and the media needs to understand that like the rest of us.

In the meantime, I would feel a lot better if Conrad Fink would assure us that our journalism colleges aren't spawning a bunch of Loren Jenkins clones but, rather, reporters and editors we can trust to show good judgment and common sense. After all, they do work for us.

Fink thinks the American public needs more information. What the American public needs is more confidence that the media will provide that information responsibly. At this time, we clearly have more faith in our government than we do in our media. For that, you can blame the media, Professor, not us.

Sound Counsel from a Tech Professor

November 19, 2001

My daddy used to say, "You don't have to be smart; you just have to recognize who is smarter than you." My friends at Georgia Tech—and believe it or not, I do have a few—will be pleased to learn that I now publicly bow in deference to one of their own. (My Tech friends will no doubt hasten to add that all their graduates and 99 percent of the flora and fauna on the planet are smarter than me, but that story is for another day.)

Everybody has been trying to cope with what happened to us on and since September 11. Buildings and airplanes and innocent lives have been blown apart and our own sense of security with them. We are equal parts mad and frustrated as to what to do next.

Enter W. J. Blane, an assistant professor of architecture at Georgia Tech.

What was I doing consorting with the enemy? I was making a speech to the Mechanical Contractors of Georgia, which seated me at Professor Blane's table for dinner. Talk, as it inevitably does these days, focused on current events and gave those of us around the table the opportunity to vent about the dire times in which we find ourselves.

Professor Blane finally put it all in marvelous perspective for us: Things have changed. Learn to live with it. Learn to deal with it. Understand what is and quit looking back to what once was. I am sure this logic has been stated before, but I have been too busy pontificating to listen. This time I was listening, and the good professor was absolutely correct. It is time to move on.

Tragically, we may never again know the tranquility and security we have enjoyed most of our lives. Tragically, our children and grandchildren and the generations to follow may live in an environment where terrorism is commonplace. Living is going to be a lot riskier than ever before. We just have to learn to deal with it.

If you are afraid to die, then you are going to have a miserable life ahead of you. If you take each day as though it truly may be your last and live it to the fullest, you will find life a lot more worthwhile. The sky will seem bluer. Your food will taste better. You will laugh more and squabble less. You will hug more and shrug less. You will learn that life's little irritations aren't worth your time. You will have more important things to do like love your family and appreciate your friends. Who knows, you might even find time to forgive a person or two for slights, real or imagined.

I have always enjoyed Thanksgiving Day and occasionally have paused between mouthfuls of turkey to remember how good I have it. From now on, I am going to try to make every day Thanksgiving Day. I am going to thank my family for putting up with my foibles and frailties. I am going to thank every police officer and firefighter I see for protecting me, sometimes even from myself. I am going to thank April, the World's Greatest Postal Worker, who cheerfully delivers a bunch of mail that usually goes straight into the trashcan. I am going to thank Dr. Gil Watson, the World's Greatest Preacher, for trying to save my wretched soul when lesser men would have given up long ago.

I am going to thank a group of people I never see for picking up our trash before dawn and never waking us while they do it. And Rick, who cuts our grass and trims our yard and makes it look better than I ever could if I spent all day, every day at it. And Ronnie, who makes our cars run because we don't know how. And my patient friends who endure me on a golf course, despite the fact that I never practice and expect to hit every shot perfectly and get mad when I don't, which is often. And those of you who don't hesitate to write me when you agree or disagree with something I have opined on these pages. Either way, you care enough to speak out.

Finally, I am going to thank Georgia Tech Professor W.J. Blane for his extremely wise counsel and for making my daddy look as smart as I always thought he was.

Struggle
for Diversity
at UGA

Bingo! Dr. Michael Adams, president of the University of Georgia, has put the responsibility of increasing student body diversity at UGA right where it belongs—on the rest of us. This is not the university's problem; it's ours.

For several years now, Dr. Adams and others have wrestled with the issue of whether UGA should take only the brightest and best from our state, which tends to make the university mostly white and predominately female, or should it more closely represent the demographics of the state, which is almost one-third minority.

UGA's minority enrollment is currently about 6 percent. That is well within the range of other state universities in the country, although that fact isn't generally made known by those who accuse the university of not trying hard enough to recruit minority students. Students who qualify to attend the University of Georgia generally have their pick of schools from which to choose. Just as every qualified white student doesn't pick UGA, neither does every qualified black student. But currently there are more qualified white students than there are qualified blacks, and that is the crux of the problem.

In comments published recently in the Atlanta newspapers, Dr. Adams said if we want more minority students in the university, society is going to have to do a better job of preparing them for college. If not, the student body will never come close to reflecting the demographics of the state.

Neither UGA nor any other institution of higher education can do in four years what elementary and secondary education failed to do in twelve. And it isn't the fault of K-12, either. The buck stops in every home of every student in the state. A good education is available to anybody who wants it. The problem is, not enough do.

But be forewarned: Education gives people the power to think and act for themselves. An educated black populace would be the worst thing that could happen to demagogues like Jesse Jackson and all the race-based organizations who need people to feel helpless and hopeless if they are to thrive as power brokers and make a few shekels in the process.

If you don't think that the black power brokers are a bunch of two-faced hypocrites, look at their obvious silence at the fact that two of the most prominent members of the Bush administration are minority success stories: Secretary of State Colin Powell and Condoleezza Rice, the president's national security advisor. I don't know about you, but I would be a tad concerned if these were "token" appointments since they hold my life in their hands. They are there because they are imminently qualified. Check their backgrounds and you will find that both took advantage of the opportunity for a good education.

Powell and Rice should be held up proudly as role models for every young black person in the country who aspires to a better life, but they hardly rate a mention from Jackson and others who profess to have their people's best interest at heart. Yeah, right. The only interest this crowd has is maintaining power, even if it means crippling an entire generation of people.

Blacks have suffered under a terrible yoke of discrimination in the "separate but equal" nonsense that was allowed to fester too many years in our society. The result has been a two-tiered society of haves and have-nots. That chasm must be eliminated, and a good education is the great equalizer. But somebody has to convince young blacks that school is "cool" or they will find themselves living on the lower end of the economic scale for the rest of their lives. No amount of demagoguery is going to change that fact.

Hopefully, there is a light at the end of this bleak tunnel. A recent Black Entertainment Television survey showed that 42 percent of the respondents said that the single biggest threat to black progress is a lack of education. Maybe that obvious point is finally getting through to some people. I hope so.

I want to see my university as diverse as it can possibly be, but I don't want to see it dumbed down just to accommodate an artificial number, and I don't want to see the courts monkeying around in the issue. Mike Adams is right as rain. Give him a large pool of qualified minority students and he'll turn out some outstanding citizens. Otherwise, we'll be fighting this battle when Jesse Jackson is just a bad memory.

What if
They Cloned
More Lawyers?   December 3, 2001

While the world was busy marveling at how the Georgia Bull-dogs kicked Georgia Tech's backsides, 31-17, and won undisputed bragging rights for a whole year (you knew I was going to sneak that in, didn't you?), scientists at Advance Cell Technology in Worcester, Massachusetts, announced that they have cloned a human embryo. As near as I can figure, they don't plan to make a bunch of new humans to tend all the sheep they have already cloned. I think they just want to turn out a few body parts.

This development raises some significant moral and ethical issues. For example, what if the Taliban had discovered that back-bones and guts could be cloned? They could have used a large quantity of both since they couldn't back up their big jivetalk about what they were going to do to the infidels. Now these brave war-riors are trying to convince us that they were only joshing and really didn't know anybody was going to take them seriously. They probably wish somebody would clone us a sense of humor.

Had cloning been possible back in the dark ages, I might have been a better student. I must confess I flunked biology in college, took it over and made a D, which matched my trigonometry and French grades. If the folks at Worcester could have given me a brain—since God didn't see fit to do so—I might have learned the difference between a hypothalamus and a hippopotamus. I know one of them lives in a river, but I can't remember which one. I would have been able to satisfy my French instructor when he asked me if a table is masculine or feminine. (I told him I'd peek under the table and see. He didn't like that answer.) I might have understood what distinguishes a tangent and a cosine, although no brain—no matter how big—could possibly figure out any rea-son to apply that piece of useless knowledge to everyday life.

Despite their claims, I suspect these scientists are pulling our uncloned leg a bit. Let's face it. If you can make a hipbone or an ear lobe, probably you can make all the other parts and put a human being together, which raises a big question of whether or not any rules exist about who or what gets cloned. For example, suppose somebody decides to make more lawyers? Lord knows, we have more now that we can possibly use. So far, we've been able to convince many of them to go into politics, which keeps them busy and out of our hair, but we may be living on borrowed time.

And do we really need to create more people driving SUVs? If so, I hope we can clone a few thousand more police officers to stop just the ones doing 95 miles per hour on the freeways, which is most of them. Who knows? We could collect enough in fines to build our own clone factory and not have to bother those snoots up in Massachusetts.

We had better think this cloning business through very carefully. What if there were two Monica Lewinskys? (Although I know somebody who might like that.) Or an additional Cynthia McKinney running loose, heaven forbid? We don't need to clone more ice hockey players, either. We need to get rid of the ones we already have.

We also don't need to clone any Brenau University graduates who have degrees in psychology and business from that outstanding university and who never attended the University of Georgia (hint, hint) running down up escalators in airports and disrupting air traffic on the eastern seaboard just to get to a football game. (If Tech fans continue to associate him with UGA, I'll remind them that when they couldn't beat the University of Maryland on the football field, they tried to beat up the band. That ought to keep them quiet for a while.)

But here is the scariest thought of all. What if somebody's bright idea is to clone The Woman Who Shares My Name? If that happens, the world will be reduced to outlet malls, two-for-one coupons, broccoli and asparagus on every dinner plate, and an outright refusal to learn to use the computer. What's more, husbands will never be allowed to make any substantive decisions or eat red meat. Is that the kind of world we want to live in?

Progress isn't necessarily a good thing.

Of Squirrels, Nuts, and BB Guns

December 10, 2001

In the short time I have been in the column-writing business, I have learned that strong opinions evoke strong reactions. When you agree, you let me know quickly and when you don't, I find that out in a hurry, too. For example, one reader reacted to my comments last week by suggesting I give up this space permanently and "go fishing." A great idea—the fishing part, I mean.

My sources tell me the journalism professors at the University of Georgia are still harrumphing after I suggested they quit worrying about how the United States conducts the war on terrorism and spend more of their time trying to restore the confidence of the American people in the integrity of the media, which is a little wobbly right now. Their reaction was to attack the messenger instead of the message. They not only missed me, they missed the point.

But nothing prepared me for the underhanded and nefarious reaction of the squirrel lobby. A few months back, I reported on efforts to rid my birdfeeders of squirrels so my feathered friends could reclaim what is rightfully theirs. Many readers sent suggestions as to how to outsmart the little varmints but, frankly, some solutions would have taken NASA scientists to implement. I had already decided to employ the most direct method possible—a genuine Red Ryder BB gun. The results have been mixed, to put the best face on the situation.

At first, I could squeeze off a few shots at the squirrels before they ran. Then the critters would scamper when they heard the back door open. Now they begin a mass exodus when they hear the key in the lock that opens the back door. Frustration and tension abound on all sides. I can't get off a shot and the squirrels can't eat in peace.

While I was busy consoling the national media because the United States seems to be winning the war handily without their help, the squirrels were taking their case to Washington. Lo and behold, the ever-vigilant folks at the Consumer Product Safety Commission have filed suit against Daisy Manufacturing Company, which produces Red Ryder, declaring that the gun is unsafe. Obviously, they accepted the squirrels' word without taking the time to watch me shoot. The only things unsafe in my yard are the hydrangeas, which are about fifteen feet from the birdfeeders. I rarely ever miss them.

No one ever said squirrels aren't sly and crafty little beasts. They recognized before any of the rest of us that the brave warriors of the Taliban can't walk the talk and as soon as the good guys could locate Osama bin Laden and Sheik Omar Whoever, our government would have a lot of free time on its hands to worry about me and all the 12-year-olds in the country who own BB guns.

The squirrels also capitalized on a political reality. The instigator of the lawsuit, Commission Chair Ann Brown, is a big-time consumer professional who probably never shot a Red Ryder in her life. If anybody knows anything about nuts, it is squirrels, and if you want somebody liable to do something totally nutty, find a big-time consumer professional with too much time on her hands.

Brown and her fellow nuts on the Consumer Product Safety Commission announced they were filing the lawsuit because BBs might get stuck in the barrel and kids might think the gun was unloaded and might not have a daddy like mine who gravely predicted every time I picked up my Red Ryder as a kid that I was going to shoot my eye out. The one dissenter among the commissioners, Mary Sheila Gall, said the CPSC hadn't been able to replicate the defect they claim makes Red Ryders dangerous. The other commissioners said it might happen anyway. Given that logic, Osama bin Laden might get plastic surgery and end up looking like Brad Pitt. Maybe Brad Pitt needs to sue all the plastic surgeons, just to be on the safe side.

If the Consumer Product Safety Commission suit is successful, some 7.5 million Red Ryders will be recalled. Make that 7,499,999. My Red Ryder isn't going anywhere. I won't be intimidated by a bunch of squirrels or a bunch of nuts in Washington. If they want war, they've got it. I just hope they will stand over by the hydrangeas so that Red and I have a fighting chance.

Everything Else Is Really Small Stuff

December 17, 2001

This is not the column I intended to write.

As I was scribbling away on another piece that would amuse my friends and confound my detractors, I learned of a family that had just lost a daughter in an automobile accident. I don't know the family, but a friend does. The young woman was an honors graduate of the University of Georgia's music department and was on her way to perform in a Christmas program of some sort when she was killed. The tragedy doesn't end there. Two years and one week ago, the family's only other child, also a daughter, was killed in an automobile accident.

While most of us are fretting over Christmas shopping, the BCS polls or some equally trivial matter, two parents will spend the rest of their lives without the people who matter most to them— their children. I cannot conceive of the pain they must feel, but the situation raises a lot of questions for which I have no answers.

What benefit accrues from losing innocent young people who have so much potential ahead of them? What higher purpose is served when crazy, immoral scum hijack airplanes and kill innocent people while half the world looks the other way or tries to justify this insanity? Why does this young woman lose her life while a dirtbag like John Walker, who turned his back on his own country and joined the Taliban, is spared? Is our world better because a good person died young and a lowlife like John Walker survives? Why couldn't it be the other way around?

Does this world really benefit from an Al Sharpton spewing his racial prejudices or a Pat Robertson blathering his narrow-minded and bigoted philosophies? In these traumatic times, wouldn't we all be better off with someone who could make a little music and for just a few minutes drown out all the smug, self-righteous elitists who want to remind us of all the things that are wrong with us?

Do we need Madonna or Eminem? Do they make our planet a

kinder and gentler and better place because they are here? And why has Osama bin Laden been allowed to walk on this earth instead of Jim Ellenberg? Jim was a quiet, humble individual and one of my best friends. Aside from my father, Jim may have been the finest man I have ever known. He died over 20 years ago, and I still miss him. I don't understand why someone that good couldn't have stayed around a little longer so that he could have touched more lives like he touched mine. And I don't understand why one family should lose both their children in automobile accidents in such a short period of time. More than enough sorry people are walking around. Why do we have to give up the good ones?

I am at a loss to understand why things happen like they do. I can only assume that God has a game plan that doesn't require my understanding or approval. It is what it is.

Instead of trying to make sense of seemingly senseless events, maybe we should spend more time trying to be better people. Maybe God is saying that when someone good leaves this earth, we need to be ready to step in and take their place, like athletes who bust their tails on the practice field in hopes that one day they'll have a chance to show that they belong on the starting team.

A good place to begin would be with placing things in the proper perspective. Certainly, my own problems don't look nearly as important as when I started writing a few hours ago. I have friends. I have family. I have four grandsons whom I love dearly. In the light of what this young woman's family is enduring, I can't think of anything that qualifies as a problem at my house anymore.

If this tragedy is God's way of telling us not to sweat the small stuff, it worked. When the good die young, everything else is really, really small stuff.

Hardly Anyone
Trusts the
Media

Over the past month, I have made a number of speeches around the state. The endeavor was time-intensive but well worth the effort. Nothing beats face-to-face communication.

I am not a demographer so my research may be statistically flawed, but I am satisfied that the people I have spoken to over the past few weeks represent a good cross section of rank-and-file Americans. My audiences were young and old, black and white, male and female. Through their questions and comments, I have a better idea of what is on their minds. Many are readers of this space, so I already had an inkling of how they felt about things before I showed up.

Nothing brought a stronger reaction from my audiences than their view of the media. The people I talked to simply don't trust the media. They think the media are biased, which is why they didn't want the *Washington Post* and the *New York Times* and ABC mucking around in the caves of Afghanistan. They don't think the media are interested in doing a fair and balanced job of reporting on the war, but, rather, engaging in a game of "gotcha" with the Bush Administration.

This news is not good. The media serve a critical role in our society of protecting citizens from the potential abuses of government, but they seem to have lost touch with the American public—certainly the people with whom I talked. The media and the people who teach journalism students need to be concerned and need to get serious about restoring the public's confidence. Otherwise, the people and groups who would like to throttle a free press are going to have a good shot at it one of these days, and the public isn't going to give a damn. I find that prospect frightening.

People are outspoken in their conviction that natural gas deregulation is an unmitigated disaster and that Bubba McDonald and the boys at the Public Service Commission have done a lousy job of managing a lousy idea. If you have a yen to run for public office, you might want to offer for the Public Service Commission when the next election rolls around. It should be easy pickings. I suspect even Mullah Omar Whatshisname would have a reasonable chance of being elected to the PSC, given the way people are feeling right now.

Osama bin Laden and the zealots associated with him are viewed as nuttier than a bunch of Claxton fruitcakes, and people are delighted to see them exposed for what they really are—cowards that couldn't walk their big talk. Not surprisingly, President Bush and his team have strong support for how they are conducting the war effort. This can't be good news for the late-night comedians, special interest groups and media pundits who believe they have a divine right to tell us how we should feel.

Police officers and firefighters can't take the following comment to the bank, but they are finally reaping the public respect they have long deserved. In my speeches, I talked about heroes. Before September 11, if you could hit a ball with a stick or if you put a plastic bowl on your head and knocked other people down—and pranced and preened a bit when you did—you were a hero. If you could sing or dance or act, you were a hero. No more. We know now that heroes dig through rubble for innocent victims and scour caves for bad guys. Heroes are Boy Scout leaders and schoolteachers, preachers and EMTs. Heroes give blood and deliver meals to shut-ins. They build houses for Habitat for Humanity. They organize walks to raise money for breast cancer research. They don't make headlines or big bucks for their efforts. They do it because it is the right thing to do, a uniquely American trait. I saw a lot of heroes in the places where I spoke, and it felt good.

In summary, the people I talked to are solid, decent Americans. They want to live their lives in peace and wish that everyone else could, too. I am glad I took the time to speak to them and wish some other media people and Public Service Commissioners and ballplayers would deign to do the same. They just might learn something useful. I did.

Who's First, Customers or Shareholders?

I usually leave economics lessons to the professors, but I feel compelled to state an untold truth about the deregulatory environment in our country: Deregulation isn't necessarily in your interest. Deregulating industries and markets is in the interest of the corporations, their largest customers and people who own the company's stock. (Everybody who wanted natural gas deregulated, please raise your hand.)

In the early days following the breakup of the Bell System, a group of Baby Bell CEOs met with a member of Congress to plead for less regulation. The congressman was clearly dubious and asked what new services the companies would offer their customers if freed of regulatory restraints. There was a short pause, and then one executive blurted out, "Whatever would make us money." Give him high marks for being honest, even if not politically astute.

I was in Washington during the days when airline deregulation was being rammed through Congress, amid glowing predictions from economists and industry executives about how unfettered competition among the airlines would benefit the American public. Fritz Hollings, the irascible senator from South Carolina, was totally unconvinced. The day the law goes into effect, Hollings said, the airlines will drop small cities from their routes and concentrate on the largest markets. History has proven Hollings more right than wrong.

Am I advocating more government control of private industry? Absolutely not. We already have more government bureaucrats than we have tasks for them to do. I am saying that as much as we all would like for things to be black or white, deregulation has a lot of gray in it. It isn't all bad but it isn't all good, either.

When we deregulate our airlines, our trucks, and our gas, electricity, telephone and cable services and let the free market work, three things tend to happen. First, as Senator Hollings correctly predicted, deregulated businesses tend to follow the Willie Sutton economic theory. Sutton, a notorious gangster of the 1930s was asked why he robbed banks. "Because," he said, "that is where the money is." In the deregulatory world, companies make more money from large commercial customers, and companies would rather ply their trade in the Atlantas of the world than the Hahiras. Shareholders, many of them large institutions, are looking for bottom-line results. That, friends, is the bottom line.

Second, while the clarion cry of those companies pushing for deregulation is "more customer choice," fewer companies are offering us fewer choices these days. The seven Baby Bells brought forth from Ma Bell in the bright promise of telecommunications competition just 18 short years ago are now four, with two-thirds of the local phone lines in the country under the control of two companies—Verizon and SBC—and more consolidation is certain in the future. Cable systems, freed from regulatory pressures, are raising rates faster than they are raising the quality of their customer service. Our choice of airlines has diminished to a handful of carriers who dominate the major hubs, controlling prices and discouraging competition.

Third, in their enthusiasm to increase profits and satisfy their shareholders, companies will enter businesses about which they know little, if anything. Witness the plethora of marketers that fell on their collective faces after promising us the moon when the natural gas fiasco began. Witness AT&T's less-than-impressive foray into cable television. Two decades ago, The Phone Company was the very model of superb service, as well as being a good citizen in every city and hamlet it served. Today, AT&T is fighting for its corporate life, and you and I aren't necessarily better off for it.

The genie is out of the bottle. Deregulation is here to stay. But industry needs to level with us when they talk about the benefits of deregulation, which is primarily for their stockholders and their big customers. The rest of us are somewhere down the food chain.

A newspaper reporter recently asked the CEO of a corporation that is vigorously pursuing deregulation how he would determine if his company would make further acquisitions. His answer was telling. "At the end of the day," he was quoted as saying, "will your shareholders be better off?" Not the customers. The shareholders. Willie Sutton would have been proud.

"Irrelevant"
Does Not Mean
"Excellent"

A friend once asked my advice about running for a seat on his county commission. I strongly urged him not to. I suggested instead that if he wanted to get into politics, he consider the state Legislature. "If you are a county commissioner, your constituents will call you every time a streetlight goes out, there is a pothole in the road or their garbage isn't picked up promptly," I told him. "If you are in the Legislature, nobody will know or care." I gave him that advice more than 20 years ago.

I thought about that conversation as I read a just-released poll from the *Atlanta Journal-Constitution* that says that more than eight out of ten citizens of metropolitan Atlanta think that the Georgia Legislature is irrelevant in their lives. Had the AJC chosen to survey the state instead of just the Atlanta area, I suspect the numbers would have been pretty much the same.

Of course, the respondents are incorrect. The Georgia Legislature is extremely relevant. They have a major say in how our children are educated. They make rules and regulations regarding the air we breathe and the water we drink. They see that highways are built and maintained and policed. They decide how our health care is provided. They also tax us. I would say that stuff is pretty relevant.

I think what those people polled are really saying is that, as a collective body, the Legislature doesn't give a flying fig about what you and I think. A typical example of their arrogance is the way they handled redistricting this past year. The whole exercise was predicated on keeping the Democrats in power until the next redistricting session ten years hence. Nothing that you and I could have done would have made a modicum of difference in the predetermined outcome. When people say the Legislature is irrelevant, they mean that the legislators clearly put their own interests ahead of their constituents'.

Let me hasten to add that many good, honest, hard-working

men and women hold a place in the Georgia Legislature. The problem is that most don't have any clout because of a system that allows a few members to wield almost absolute power over the rest. The powers that be are known as the Green Door Committee, and it is the most exclusive of clubs. Unless this group says "okay," you couldn't get a bill passed extolling the virtues of motherhood and apple pie. The poster boy for this little clique is, of course, House Speaker Tom Murphy.

Veteran political observer Bill Shipp says Murphy is in his Last Hurrah, but before he lights up one last cigar and toodles off into the Haralson County sunset, he is trying to decide who to beknight as his successor, House Majority Leader Larry Walker (D-Perry) or House Appropriations Chairman Terry Coleman (D-Eastman). Shipp says Murphy wants whoever becomes Speaker to appoint the other one chairman of the appropriations committee. I know you are all a-twitter over how this scene will play out. If you are putting together an office pool on the subject, let me give you a heads-up. It doesn't matter who becomes Speaker. The same clique will still be in place with a new poster boy at its head. They will continue to pass whatever bills suit them and scuttle any that don't, and they will continue to do business with state agencies, if they so chose.

That kind of environment spawned the opinions in the *Atlanta Journal-Constitution* survey. Maybe the Legislature thinks we are too dumb to understand how they operate. If so, they are mistaken. We are smart enough to know that no matter how hard we press our representatives or senators, they can't do diddly-squat without the approval of the Speaker and the Green Door Committee. So, we shrug and go on with our lives.

Speaker-hopeful Larry Walker has a different slant on the poll results. He told the Atlanta newspapers the numbers "simply prove that we're doing an excellent job." His logic seems to be that it is only when constituents are angry that they think about the Legislature, and because our elected officials are doing such bang-up work on our behalf, we tend to get complacent and forget they are there. If he really believes that is what the poll is saying, those guys behind the Green Door are smoking something stronger than Tom Murphy's cigars.

Mayor Franklin
Can Revive
Atlanta's Vision

January 28, 2002

A question I am asked quite often these days is what I think of Shirley Franklin, the new mayor of Atlanta. The answer is, I think she is terrific. She and I worked together at the Atlanta Committee for the Olympic Games. We both reported directly to Billy Payne, ACOG's CEO. We both were impatient, opinionated and outspoken, and we got along famously. As we say down South, she is good folks.

A more important question that people should be asking is, if you don't live within the city limits of Atlanta, why should you care about Shirley Franklin or the city? The short answer is that the Atlanta she has inherited is in a state of chaos and financially unable to fix its own problems. Enter the State of Georgia and your pocketbook.

Thanks to inept management by the administration of Mayor Bill Campbell over the past eight years, the city has almost ground to a halt. Hartsfield International Airport is a mess. So is the Metropolitan Atlanta Rapid Transit Authority. So are the city's roads and sewers and water and air. Atlanta can do little to address these issues in the near future because the city is also some $85 million in debt. Increasing taxes won't cover this shortfall because the city is too poor. The idea of taxing commuters who come into the city will never see the light of day. But you can bet Aunt Ellie's calf that the State of Georgia will find some way to provide financial support to Atlanta—with your tax dollars. The city is too important to the state and to the Democratic Party to do otherwise.

What Atlanta needs as much as state support is leadership. Currently the city is devoid of any leadership of any kind from anybody. No one in the business community had any influence with Bill Campbell, primarily because they were afraid of him and the race card that he would play anytime it suited his purposes, which was often. But, of course, the local moguls would never admit their fear. One CEO dressed me down in front of a group of colleagues for even suggesting such a thing. Ironically, his company is now very much in disfavor with the city. So much for influence.

Perhaps most culpable for the city's lack of leadership are the local news media. Now that Bill Campbell is out of office, they have finally decided that maybe he didn't do such a good job as mayor. Duh! During the planning period for the 1996 Games, I urged the newspapers to use their influence to see that the city was ready for the billions of people around the world who would be watching us during the Games. Instead, they preferred to second-guess the Committee and spent countless column inches on such flaming issues as our woebegone mascot, Izzy. As a result, Atlanta looked like a cheap flea market during the Olympics. The Games were good. The city was not. The media are largely to blame.

Mayor Shirley Franklin can provide the leadership that has been missing in Atlanta. It won't be easy. She must address some serious questions beyond the city's financial and operational problems. First and foremost, what role will former mayor and current bond lawyer Maynard Jackson play behind the scenes of a Franklin administration? The new mayor makes no apologies for her friendship with Jackson, whom she credits as her mentor. Whether he will exert his considerable influence in the city's business remains to be seen.

How will she handle the enormous racial divide that grips the city? The politically potent Concerned Black Clergy has little to gain in seeing the city become whiter and more prosperous. Such a move would seriously diminish their power, and they aren't about to let that happen.

Can Franklin improve the quality of life in the city? If so, she is going to have to face down the do-gooders who are more concerned with protecting the rights of the homeless and the panhandlers than in assuring people they can go downtown without being harassed or threatened.

Clearly, Atlanta Mayor Shirley Clarke Franklin has her work cut out for her. I wish her all the best and I suggest you keep an eye on her progress no matter where you live in the state because your tax dollars might be needed to help her succeed.

Just for the Record: My Résumé

Dear Boss:

You are no doubt up-to-date on the latest incident of resume padding at Georgia Tech. The new assistant football coach, Rick Smith, has confessed that he didn't play football or baseball at Florida State as his résumé claims. Happily, the good folks at Tech have told him not to worry about the oversight. They have had some experience with this sort of thing in the past.

However, I suggest that we stay ever vigilant and not let any more people skate by with puffing up their résumés with fictitious accomplishments just to land a job. You can rest assured that I am on the case and eager to assist in uncovering any future examples of misfeasance or malfeasance or whatever you call saying you did something you didn't do.

Before I join this crusade, I do need to make a couple of small, technical changes to my own résumé . Unlike what has happened at Georgia Tech, most folks would not even notice these are really minor things, but I don't think it would look good for me to be actively exposing résumé rogues if even a scintilla of inaccuracy appeared in my own materials.

First off, I didn't actually win a Medal of Honor as my résumé states but I have seen every movie that John Wayne made. *Flying Leathernecks* was my all-time favorite.

On one of my previous résumé s, I recall saying that I was a member of the Georgia General Assembly. I figured most people in the state wouldn't care enough to check that out and that I could get a lot of free lunches from the lobbyists and might even get elected Speaker of the House. But then, I figured I needed to protect whatever little reputation I have, so I took that out.

And then there is that pesky reference to the Nobel Prize for Literature. I am a little sensitive about that one. I wrote a book on the 1996 Olympics entitled, *And They Call Them Games*. I wasn't very nice to the Atlanta newspapers and they, in turn, refused to review my book—the only one written on the biggest event to hit Atlanta since General Sherman came to town—saying it was "not of general interest." I have no doubt that cost me the Nobel Prize and if you have no objection, I would like to leave that one in my résumé . I think I was robbed.

I am willing, however, to drop the mention of the Oscar. Admittedly, I became a little carried away about my acting performance when I was stopped by a Laurens County deputy for driving 71 in a 55 mph zone. With equal amounts of charm and humility, I managed to avoid a ticket. The county mountie went back to his patrol car thinking he had just had a conversation with Jimmy Stewart. I was that good.

If senior counselor to the University of Georgia bothers you, we can talk about this one, but I think it is pretty accurate. Everybody who knows me knows that I give unsolicited advice to anyone I can lay my hands on at UGA, including President Mike Adams and Athletic Director Vince Dooley. I also spend a lot of time at the Journalism College suggesting how the professors raise up the next generation of reporters. It is a wonderful service that I offer my alma mater and I do it for free. As to how successful I have been, I really can't tell you, although one of the journalism professors recently called me a "flack," which means somebody must be listening.

Finally, you will notice the reference to my having played three years of football at the University of New Hampshire, while getting my master's at NYU. I decided that at this advanced stage of my career it would be fun to be the head football coach at Notre Dame and I thought a slight exaggeration wouldn't hurt anything. Now, I am ashamed of myself, not for having put it on my résumé , but that George O'Leary thought of it before I did.

I promise I will clean up my résumé promptly and send you a new copy so that never again will you have to worry about the accuracy of my background. Thanks for your understanding.

Dick Yarbrough
Member, Order of the British Empire
and former Apollo astronaut

Rosie Inspires
Me to 'Fess Up

If Rosie O'Donnell can do it, so can I.

In case you have been busy with mundane stuff like making a living, you may have missed the big news that has the entertainment world in a dither. The popular daytime television talk show host will apparently come out of the closet and proclaim her sexuality. To borrow some show business lingo, Rosie is "outing herself."

The smart money says she is going to declare she is gay. Whatever she does it will be a huge relief because once she says whatever she's going to say, we can move on with our lives. I don't know about you, but wherever I go—be it to the hardware store or Benny's BP station—this is the only thing people are talking about.

Rosie O'Donnell's decision places an obligation on the rest of us to undergo a little soul searching of our own. For too many years, I have avoided the subject, but I feel I no longer have that option. After many sleepless nights of wrestling with my own conscience, the time has come for me to out myself.

I am straight.

I am not sure when my tendencies first began to show, but one of my earliest memories is how my heart thumped when I saw Margaret Pittman in the third grade. I had a lot of male friends in the third grade, but none of them looked anywhere near as good as Margaret. In the middle of the year, I was moved to another grammar school. To this day, I don't know if the move happened because my parents were embarrassed about my preference for girls, but the change was a total failure. I promptly fell in love with Christine Shellnut.

Other signs were obvious, too, if you knew what to look for. I used to dress up like boys. I had a crew cut, wore black high-top Keds and had holes in the knees of all my blue jeans. I played ball and rode bicycles and came home dirty. I learned to scratch and spit. My poor parents must have been mortified at my behavior. Naturally, I became more rebellious as I grew older and even married a person of the opposite sex. Little did I know at the time what ground I was breaking.

Somehow I never thought of myself as a pioneer but just a guy who was being true to his own yin and yang. Yet, I could never muster the courage to come out of the workroom in my garage and publicly confess. Coming out of the closet was never an option for me because all of our closets are full of clothes that someone who shares my name can't bring herself to throw away.

No doubt I'll pay a high price to pay for outing myself. I haven't told my partner of 43 years, although I think she has been suspicious about me from the beginning.

I can forget being invited to the next national Democratic Party celebrity fund-raiser in Hollywood. No way are Democrats going to want a straight white guy hanging around with all the movie stars and rappers.

I'll watch out for other repercussions as well. Don't look for Elton John to perform at our Sunday school party next Christmas, although—come to think of it—I don't believe he has come to any of our Sunday school parties in the past. I guess we can forget Ellen Degeneres, too.

But if I am anything, I am a fighter. Now that I am out, the first thing I am going to do is join a straight rights group and protest the popular television sitcom about a gay man, *Will and Grace*. Admittedly, this tactic is not new. I am shamelessly borrowing from the playbook of gay rights groups who intimidated stations into not carrying the *Dr. Laura* syndicated television show. I'm not sure how much success we will have because straights only make up about 90 percent of the population, but we have to start somewhere.

I fervently hope that my example will inspire others to admit they are straight. Maybe my golfing buddies at Sea Island will emerge from their lives of quiet torment. Straight is okay. I used to think I could never discuss a sensitive subject like this publicly, but thanks to Rosie, I can and I have and I feel terrific.

How in the world was Tony Cole ever accepted to the University of Georgia? To refresh your memory, Cole is one of three UGA athletes being investigated for having raped a female student or having had consensual sex with her or some combination of both, depending on whose story you believe.

Call me naïve, but I was hoping someone would say that Cole was attracted to Athens by the new School of Public and International Affairs and decided to get a head start on things by having a very public and international affair in his dorm room one night last January. But I think the truth is that he is here because of his considerable talents as a basketball player.

Admittedly, I have never met the young man, but anyone who went to five different high schools and prep schools from Maine to California as well as to two community colleges, who didn't have the grades to get into the University of Rhode Island, and who is developing a higher profile as a sexual miscreant than as a ball handler had to look like trouble from the get-go.

I don't blame basketball coach Jim Harrick for bringing Tony Cole to the University of Georgia. Harrick was hired to win games and obviously he thinks that Cole can help him do that. Rather, I blame those of us who call ourselves boosters. We applaud politely about the rising academic standards at Athens and we mean it, up to a point. But deep in our hearts we have a burning desire to consistently beat Tennessee and Florida and Georgia Tech. If it means going out on the margins and recruiting academically challenged athletes, then we say go do it. Besides, we rationalize, all the other schools do that, so why not us?

Gone are the days when athletic success was defined as winning a majority of your season's games. Now, you have to win the conference championship and have a legitimate shot at a national championship to keep the natives happy and the sportswriters off your back. And if you are going to win consistently these days, you have to be willing to deal with a lot of kids who may be good athletes but bad character risks.

It disturbs me that my alma mater has to put up with this kind of wrong-headed thinking from a lot of alumni and from people who never spent one day in school at UGA. Having labored in the university's fundraising vineyards for more than a few years, I can state without hesitation that the people who yell the loudest about the performance of the ball teams give the least amount of money to the university in general or they give no money at all. These people don't care as much about SATs as they do PATs.

The rising academic level at the university is attracting so many excellent students that Athens hasn't enough space for them all. But a good shooter or deft dribbler or snappy passer? Come right in. Someone who bopped around the nation as a part of the School-of-the-Month program can get in UGA while a good student in Lee County can't. One can throw a no-look pass. The other one can't.

College sports aren't sports anymore. While we weren't looking, they became big business. Television calls the shots. They pay the big bucks. They tell you to play your games early in the morning or late at night; never mind the inconvenience to ticket holders. If schools don't cooperate they won't get the money or sufficient exposure to attract enough talented 18-year-old athletes who are looking for a free ride to the pros. Don't attract them and you won't win. Don't win and influential boosters will raise holy hell and make life miserable for the university.

Top-flight academic institution or national championship? Having both is damn near impossible. We have to make choices. Right now that choice seems to be an easy one for a lot of so-called supporters of the University of Georgia: Just win, baby, win. If that requires admitting a sexually overactive point guard who wouldn't know a library from a beanbag, then so be it.

Ted Has a Right
to Put His Foot
in His Mouth

Well, if I can do it, I guess Ted Turner can, too.

A week after I induced mass hyperventilation with my tongue-in-cheek spoof of television personality Rosie O'Donnell's upcoming announcement that she is gay, Ted Turner's comments at a Brown University forum made me hyperventilate a bit myself.

In case you missed it, Turner called Arab terrorists "brave" for flying airplanes into the World Trade Center and the Pentagon and killing thousands of innocent people. I was outraged with Turner's latest babbling. The brave people are the office workers trying to support their families who found themselves in the wrong place at the wrong time. The brave people are the police officers and firefighters trying to dig out and recover the bodies of the victims of this tragedy, who need a year to earn what Turner makes in a couple of hours. Those people are the brave ones, not a bunch of cowards who would rather kill than defend their philosophy. I was not assuaged at his trotting out the hoary "quoted out of context" alibi, either. He has said too many hurtful things in the past to have been misquoted.

This buffoonery is only the latest from a man who has insulted Haitians and Italians and Jews and Christians and the pope himself. Turner gets away with it because he is filthy rich. A lot of people want to dive their mitts into his money, so they give him a free ride. The Atlanta newspapers, which nearly decimated a forest savaging former Atlanta Braves pitcher John Rocker—a complete nonentity on the world scene—for his insensitive observations about New York and gays, issued a mild tut-tut to Turner for his remarks at Brown. To Rocker's credit, he was only stupid once. Turner has turned stupid into an art form.

I thought a lot about how to respond to a man that I consider several pecans short of a fruitcake. I came to the inevitable conclusion that, as much as I hate to admit it and as much as his remarks offended me, he is exercising his constitutional right of free speech.

I have those same rights and so do you. Many —maybe even most—people on this earth can't speak out the way we can. When I stated last year that the terrorists who bombed the *USS Cole* were cowards and would drop their guns and run if ever challenged, I received mail from all over the Arab world. Few writers wanted to discuss the issues behind the bombing. The majority intended to intimidate me—kind of a verbal terrorist attack. Free speech appears about as rare in the Arab world as female ice hockey.

A lot of gays found my satire about Rosie O'Donnell humorous and said so. Many didn't and they said so, too, which is fine. But no one referenced my comments about the efforts of gay rights groups to prevent television stations from running the *Dr. Laura* show because of her publicly stated anti-gay bias. That is censorship, pure and simple, and everybody ought to be concerned about their tactics, including gays. Frankly, I wouldn't watch *Dr. Laura* if you paid me good money, but I resent a small group of people keeping her off the air because they don't like what she says. I also question why the media has not made this issue more high-profile. If they won't protect free speech, who will?

What we have is an attitude creeping into our society that free speech is okay as long as it is politically correct. Maybe special interest groups are so unsure of their causes that they can't brook any criticism of it. These groups need to understand that if they intend to dish it out, they are going to have to learn to take it. The right of free speech cuts both ways.

So let Ted Turner rant to his heart's content. Let the academics, religious zealots and assorted special interest groups rage at my own musings. Turner's blathering reminded me that free speech isn't always pretty and is rarely popular, but it makes our country great. May we all exercise our rights to the fullest. Thank you, Ted. I think you are an absolute jerk, but maybe we all learned something from you last week.

When Six Months Seem an Eternity

March 11, 2002

Has it been just six months since our world was turned upside down? Was it only this past September when a bunch of madmen—not brave men, madmen—destroyed so many innocent people and forever changed the lives of the rest of us? I kept asking myself those questions last week as I listened to the students and faculty at my grandsons' school present a stirring tribute to America. The assembled experienced soaring highs as we heard patriotic songs and mind-numbing lows as we saw pictures of airplanes crashing into the World Trade Center. A lot of tears were shed that evening.

Our country has been on an emotional roller coaster since September 11. We have been reminded that the vast majority of us are good people who genuinely care about others in a generally uncaring world. Yet we have witnessed firsthand the evil of which some are capable and are amazed that people like that even exist in the twenty-first century.

Just when we think it can't get any worse, a group of Muslim extremists—who else?—captures a *Wall Street Journal* reporter and cuts off his head. What kind of people are these, we wonder, and why aren't Arabs expressing universal condemnation at such barbaric acts? Instead, they seem to prefer to complain about racial profiling. Arabs could help their case immeasurably if we heard a little more righteous indignation from them. Most of us haven't forgotten the deafening silence from the Arab world after the attacks. They would be wise to remember President Bush's admonition—you are either with us or you are against us.

Six months ago, focusing on all that is wrong with us was quite the fashion. The thought police discouraged us from openly expressing love of country. That silliness stopped with the airliner attacks. We have jumped the politically-correct fence, and the special interest groups are going to have a heck of a time herding us back in. We have found our voice. Flag waving is in. Self-flagellation

168

is out. How long this will continue, I don't know. I hope it is a long time.

So far, we seem to approve of how the president is conducting the war. We like him calling North Korea and Iraq and Iran "an axis of evil" because that is what they are. We knew the French would be critical of our president for telling the truth, and they didn't disappoint us. We start to get angry and then we remember, their government threw down their guns and quit when they saw the first German tank coming over the hill in World War II. Who cares what the French think?

We abide the hand wringing of the International Red Cross and assorted do-gooders over the "treatment" of the Taliban thugs in Guantanamo Bay and the face time the television networks give them for posturing. We wonder if these groups understand that a lot of individuals won't send them a dime in the future because their priorities are not our priorities. We also wonder why the networks don't spend equal time showing the squalid conditions our soldiers are enduring in Afghanistan.

We ignore the self-important journalists who harrumph over the audacity of the U.S. government to fight a war without their meddling. We are a peaceful people, but most of the rest of the world is too dense to understand that we have been pushed as far as we will go. We are going to have to kick some more tail before the word gets around. If the media don't approve of that, let them go hold hands with the French.

The past six months have been difficult, and the scary thing is that the years to follow could be even tougher. We have no way of knowing what will happen, but this much is certain: We can't go back and change the events of September 11 any more than we can predict the future. What we can do is to accept each day as a blessed gift and live it to the best of our abilities. And we must never, ever let one day go by without remembering the searing image of those airplanes crashing into the World Trade Center. To forget would be the ultimate insult to the people who died that day and encouragement to the thugs who wish us further harm. Don't let the bad guys think they won.

Great State, Great Song

Here is some late-breaking news you won't read anywhere else. After hours of exhaustive analysis by my crack research department, staffed by the same person who writes this column, and after intensive scientific polling, which consisted of asking the Woman Who Shares My Name if she agreed with me, I am proud to announce that the State of Georgia has been identified as the finest place on earth to live. Tied for second were the other 49 states and Scotland. Third place went to everyplace else on earth, except France, which whines too much and was automatically disqualified.

Maybe now you will realize how fortunate you are to call Georgia home. You could be living up north where it snows ten months a year or out in California where they have to schedule electrical blackouts, mudslides and earthquakes on alternate days just to get them all in.

Consider all our state has to offer: Mountains. Seashore. Good weather. Good roads. Good people. The Masters. NASCAR races. Lake Lanier. The Exquisite Little Georgia Sea Grill on St. Simons Island. Julia Roberts. Peanuts and Peaches. Our cup runneth over.

Yeah, I know we also have ice hockey, Ted Turner and natural gas deregulation, but nobody is perfect, okay?

Georgia's finest attribute, however, is our official state song, "Georgia on My Mind." No other state has a song that's even close. Not only is it the world's greatest song, it is sung by the world's greatest singer, Ray Charles, who just happens to be from Albany. Are we on a roll or what?

But the alarm bells are ringing. A columnist in Atlanta doesn't think "Georgia On My Mind" is an appropriate marketing slogan for our state. Not appropriate? We are identified with the world's greatest song and it is not appropriate? What is it with newspaper columnists who think they know everything and have to tell you, whether you want to hear it or not? (Present company excluded, of course.)

She thinks "Georgia Loves You" would be a better line to sell people on coming to Georgia. Oh, please. Not only does that put me to sleep, but also it would be downright dishonest. Georgia doesn't love everybody. Not by a long shot. For example, we don't love Osama bin Laden. Imagine bin Laden curled up in a fetal position in some stinking cave in Afghanistan saying, "I made a boo-boo last September and now everybody is mad at me. I am going to Georgia because Georgia loves me." See what a mistake that would be?

Had the columnist done the kind of in-depth research as your intrepid servant, she would have quickly discovered "Georgia Loves You" is a very bad idea. What if Al Sharpton thought we loved him and decided to move here? Or Madonna? Or Dennis Rodman? Or Alec Baldwin? Are these the kind of people we want running around loose in our state?

Not only would she have the state adopt "Georgia Loves You," but she suggests that all our cities use that same line, too. Of course, being headquartered in Atlanta she probably can't name three other cities in the state because people in Atlanta don't know there are three other cities in the state. But even Sheila, the family Wonder Dog, would have a hard time swallowing "Ludowici Loves You" or "Ty Ty Loves You." I know folks in both places and they would be very uncomfortable hearing talk like that. People are likely to think they are a bunch of Rosie O'Donnells and avoid them, which could damage tourism and hurt their chances of landing a major league baseball franchise.

Our politicians tend to forget who elected them and it is not the Atlanta media. The next time you see your local representatives—assuming the Legislature ever runs out of busy work and goes home—remind them that they are going to miss a lot of free lobbyist dinners in the future because they won't be going back to the Gold Dome if you catch them messing with either Ray Charles or "Georgia on My Mind." Tell them you don't want to give Al Sharpton the idea Georgia loves him. You don't want to go deer hunting and have folks say, "Aren't you from that town where all that lovey-dovey stuff goes on?" Remind them that if we happen to say "Georgia Loves You," we are talking only about Ray Charles—especially when he sings "Georgia on My Mind."

Thwarting
Democracy
at the Capitol
April 1, 2002

Just when we think the Legislature can't drop any lower in our collective esteem, they show us once again that there are no depths to which they can't sink. Consider the recent antics of Senator Robert Brown (D-Macon), chairman of the Senate Insurance and Labor Committee. I'm not sure how the State Senate selects their leadership, but after what Brown did, I can only assume they flip a coin or draw straws. Surely, this guy didn't land this chairmanship on merit.

Brown had a bill in his committee that would allow people who had lost their jobs due to domestic abuse to collect unemployment benefits, which sounds like a reasonable proposal to me. For reason to which I am not privy, the committee Brown chairs defeated it on a voice vote, according to a number of people who were present. That result didn't suit Chairman Brown, who declared the bill had passed and then scampered out of the room, refusing to allow a show of hands. He later claimed he had to catch a bus to Macon. Yeah, right. The Greyhound bus station is always packed in the afternoon with legislators trying to make it home before dark.

Does anybody in state government understand? Does anybody comprehend how disgusted we are with that kind of behavior? Or does anybody care what we think? First, the General Assembly rigs redistricting to accommodate their personal political needs, and then the leadership refuses to accept a legitimate vote of the representatives you and I elected because the answer the representatives gave wasn't what the leadership wanted.

The fault is ours, you know. We have become so apathetic that we have allowed a democracy of the people, by the people, and for the people to become the private province of a bunch of arrogant and self-serving politicians who think they are accountable only to Governor Roy Barnes and House Speaker Tom Murphy. You and I sit on the sidelines and tell ourselves that the whole system stinks, but we won't do anything to change it because we have come to believe that we can't. People like Robert Brown are not only reelected, but they actually serve in positions of leadership, God help us.

The reaction to Brown's underhanded methods was interesting. The Republicans, who opposed the bill, were handed a ready-made issue that they used to the best of their limited abilities. They strung up crime scene tape and made a lot of speeches about how the Democrats mistreat them. The Democrats for the most part ignored the Republicans—and Brown's actions—and went on with business as usual, which is passing whatever legislation suits them. Just another routine day under the Gold Dome.

Both sides should have come together in joint session and agreed that what happened was unconscionable and unforgivable. They should have censured that bozo of a chairman and stripped him of his position and put him on the first bus back to Macon in time for supper. Then the whole crowd—the governor, lieutenant governor, the speaker and everybody in the Legislature—should have publicly apologized to us all for abusing the responsibilities we have entrusted to them. After that, everybody could have gone back to work, knowing they had done the right thing and had gained some much needed respect from the public. The first order of business would be to debate the merits of unemployment benefits for domestic violence victims, except to go about it the right way this time.

Of course, all of the above will happen when pigs fly. If the government is a food chain of power, you and I are the amoebae. Our job is to keep mindlessly reelecting these people and then stepping out of their way so they can spend our tax dollars as they choose—subject to input from lobbyists and political consultants, of course—and with no accountability for their actions.

I have said on more than one occasion that the majority of men and women we elect to public office are honest and hard-working people intent on doing the right thing. Regrettably, they are overshadowed by the likes of Senator Robert Brown, who gives democracy a swift kick in the groin whenever the process doesn't work the way he wants it to.

The good news is that a bus is ready to take this guy to Macon. The bad news for us is that Greyhound goes both ways, and that Brown always seems to come back.

Robot Reporter
Poses Problems

Well, you knew it had to happen sooner or later. According to the Associated Press, some pointyheads at the Massachusetts Institute of Technology have begun work on a robot reporter. Evidently, our lives aren't fulfilled enough talking to recordings instead of live human beings whenever our power, telephone or cable goes haywire. Now, we are going to have some gadget running around gathering news for us.

The chief pointyhead on the project, Chris Csikszentmihalyi, is quoted as saying the intent in developing this mechanical news gatherer is to assist, not replace, human reporters. Yeah, right. That's what the techno-geeks always say. Mark my words, they won't be happy until some glass-eyed android kicks me out of this space so it can regale you with stories on Einstein's theory about his relatives.

Mr. Csikszentmihalyi, who heads the Media Lab at MIT, says that the remote-controlled robots, loaded up with accelerometers, distance sensors and cameras, could zip up to the front lines in Afghanistan and gather news and then zip back home. I am certain that this effort will have the total support of the reporters there. Robots would keep them from getting shot at and allow them more time to sit around the bar at the Kandahar Hilton and complain about their expense accounts.

Far be it for a humble UGA graduate to criticize Mr. Whoozit and the gang at MIT, but they might want to consider one slight change in their design. Current plans call for the roving robot reporter to carry a flag with a peace symbol on its antenna, signifying its neutrality. I guess it has not occurred to the geniuses that some grunt private sitting armpit deep in a muddy trench will pull out his M16 and send this marvel of technology to robot heaven when it comes chugging past him waving its little peace flag.

Still, this may be an idea whose time has come. I suspect that newspaper editors would love roving robots in their newsrooms, and why not? They wouldn't have to listen to reporters whine about deadlines and about having their stories edited. If one of the robots asked for a raise, the editor could stomp the sucker to pieces and pull a new one out of the box.

I must confess that I don't know exactly how the roving robot reporter works, but I've got to believe that if it can be made to operate in Afghanistan, it could work in other hostile environments—like the State Capitol. Of course, the rover would have to undergo a couple of modifications. If the gizmo wanted to interview Democrats, it would fly the new state flag. For Republicans, it would hoist up the old Stars and Bars banner. And if our esteemed public servants chose to ignore the little bugger's questions, it would zap their fannies good and proper with its hidden laser gun.

The roving robot reporter would undoubtedly pose a serious problem for journalism schools around the nation. Professors would have the challenge of making the machines lean to the left like the Woodward and Bernstein wannabes they crank out each year. And there is the additional concern of learning to change the robot's oil and tune up its accelerometers. Can't you just picture a journalism professor in white coveralls and safety glasses telling a student, "Mr. Figley, for the last time: That is not a spark plug. That is a crankshaft."

Am I threatened by this new technological innovation? Darn right I am. The silly thing probably knows where to put all the commas and semicolons in a column without asking and can split an infinitive as easily as it can an atom. With a tinker here and a hot wire there, a robot could even be taught to write nice things about ice hockey, the world's dumbest game, and natural gas deregulation, the world's dumbest idea.

I don't know about the rest of my colleagues, but I choose to fight back. If the boys at MIT can stick their uninvited noses in the Fourth Estate and grace us with a robot reporter, why shouldn't I reciprocate and construct a robot engineer? How hard could it be? All I need to do is slap on a couple of plastic pocket protectors and make sure it looks like a nerd.

McKinney's
Assertions
an Outrage

Our Ambassador to Outer Space has outdone herself this time. Cynthia McKinney, the loudmouth congresswoman from Georgia's Fourth District who wouldn't recognize shameful conduct if it bit her on the backside, says President Bush may have received advanced warnings of the September 11 terrorist attacks and chose to do nothing about it. If reincarnation exists, this woman is coming back as a fruit tree.

McKinney alleges the president was willing to sacrifice thousands of American lives in order to encourage a war and thereby benefit the defense industry. She asserts that the military response that followed the attacks has profited companies specializing in defense contracts, including the Carlyle Group, where President Bush's father is on the board.

On what does she base her preposterous charges of presidential malfeasance? Nothing. After blathering her conspiracy malarkey to a radio station in—where else?—Berkeley, California, home of the University of Goofyland, McKinney later issued a statement saying: "I am not aware of any evidence showing that President Bush or members of his administration have personally profited from the attacks of 9/11." The logical question, then, is why in the hell did she say it?

Her insane charges repulsed most of the Georgia delegation. Senator Zell Miller called her comments "loony." Representative Johnny Isakson, from Georgia's Seventh District, said McKinney "demonstrated a total lack of responsibility." Tenth District representative Charlie Norwood suggested ostracizing her. I would add that the delegation also should hold their noses whenever they pass her in the halls of Congress. Only Jack Kingston, the glib Republican from Georgia's First District offered McKinney any support. He is quoted as saying, "She has the right to make the statements." Yeah, and she also has the obligation to back them up with facts, Mr. Congressman, or have you been in Never-Never

Land too long yourself? I would suggest the Georgia delegation hold their nose when they pass Kingston, too.

Some observers believe McKinney is playing to the voters back home. If partisan politics has stooped to this kind of low, then let me out of here. Her kind of behavior has no place in a time of national crisis. If she was trying to impress the home folks, why didn't she come back to Georgia and make her charges? Could it be that she is contemplating a move to Goofyland and becoming their Ambassador to Outer Space? That pairing would be the most appropriate partnership since Seigfried met Roy.

Maybe her daddy, state representative Billy McKinney, and his omnipresent bullhorn could explain to us why his baby girl thinks the president of the United States purposely allowed American citizens to be killed in order to enrich American corporations. This approach has been the Ambassador to Outer Space's modus operandi: Say something totally outrageous and then hide from the media and the voters, while Daddy runs around bellowing into his bullhorn and defending her indefensible actions.

I can only assume she and Daddy believe the clueless constituents of the Fourth District will return her to Washington, no matter how much she acts like Clarabelle the Clown. Well, the gig may be over for the McKinney clan. An impressive candidate has made the decision to run against Madame Flap Jaw in the upcoming election. Denise Majette, a former State Court judge from Stone Mountain, is willing to endure the abuse the McKinneys are certain to heap on her and to give the Fourth District some relevant representation for a change. Like the incumbent, Judge Majette is a black female. This fact is going to pose a problem for Daddy and daughter, who can play a race card better than Willie Nelson can sing "Amazing Grace." But, trust me, they will find a way.

If McKinney does make it back to Washington to continue her legislative record of having done absolutely nothing worthwhile in ten years, I will be anxious to see if she can wangle her usual spot on the aisle in order to shake President Bush's hand on national television as he walks in to deliver the State of the Union speech. My fantasy is that when she sticks her hand out next time and gives him that loopy smile of hers, the president will stop and cold-cock her right on her kisser in front of the world. Now, that would be some outrageous behavior I could go for!

Stop the Press!
Tech Says
Speed Kills

My oldest grandson, Zachary, has just turned 15. (I know what you are thinking—this guy is too young to have a 15-year-old grandson. I agree.)

Zack is now eligible for his automobile learner's permit, which will allow him to drive on the Georgia autobahns with adult supervision. Fortunately, his mom and dad are good drivers and Zack is wise and possessed of abundant caution beyond his years. Still I worry.

Roughly 6 million people are licensed to drive in Georgia. Of that number, 5,999,997 drive like maniacs. Georgia is the largest state east of the Mississippi River, covering some 59,000 square miles and with over 1,200 miles of interstate highway. Yet fewer than 1,000 state patrol officers are available to protect us from each other.

Why so few state patrol personnel for so many drivers and so much territory? First, the starting salary is $28,000, which is less than what Atlanta Braves second baseman Marcus Giles makes every time he bobbles a baseball. I can't imagine many people are willing to put up with the risks of a job for that kind of money. Why don't we pay them more? Law enforcement salaries aren't a priority issue in Georgia because the Legislature has more important items to deal with, like making grits the official breakfast of champions and declaring pecans, Ted Turner, and Cynthia McKinney the state's official nuts.

Besides, if we had enough state troopers and they started cracking down on Georgia's tailgating, road-raging drivers, we would raise hell and write letters to the editor, defending our constitutional right to act like morons. That would get the Legislature stirred up because at least half of us occasionally vote. The Legislature would then take it out on the state patrol, making it even harder to convince people to work there for a whopping $28,000.

I have told Grandson Zack all of this, but I can tell that he still has questions. Why, he must wonder, do seemingly normal adults act like three-year-old brats when they step into a motor vehicle of any type? Why do generally law-abiding citizens think it is okay to routinely exceed the speed limit by 20 miles an hour, never use a turn signal while changing lanes, and run up on the back of those drivers who have the audacity to obey the speed limit? Why, in this time when a bunch of nut cases in the Middle East threaten us with an oil embargo, do we buy gas-guzzling SUVs and call ourselves patriotic?

Just when I thought these questions had no answers, here come those smart folks at Georgia Tech (Zack's favorite school, incidentally) galloping to the rescue. Tech has announced a two-year, $3.1 million study on the effects of speed in automobile accidents. The leader of the study is quoted as saying, "What we do not know is if people who are frequent speeders are more likely to crash or not." They want to recruit 1,100 speed demons to help them find out, which should be pretty easy to do, since they have 5,999,997 to choose from.

I am going out on a limb here, but having ventured onto our state's highways recently, I have this gut feeling that speeders are more likely to crash than people who observe the speed limit and that most of them drive an SUV the size of a Patton tank or an 18-wheel truck with a "How's My Driving?" bumper sticker. If my friends at Georgia Tech had asked me, I would have been happy to share this information with them free of charge and saved them $3.1 million that they could have put to better use, like recruiting running backs who don't fumble.

That leads me to this public service announcement. I love Zachary more than life itself, and if I am in the car with him and you tailgate him or cut in front of him without using your turn signal, I am going to find you and apply a stick upside your head. This announcement will no doubt give rise to another multi-million dollar study by the wizards at Georgia Tech: learning how to behave yourself and act real nice when Zachary Wansley is on the road so you don't have to face an overly protective grandfather who means what he says. Happy motoring, Zack.

BellSouth Guilty
of Nothing
But Naïveté

The road to hell is paved with good intentions. Just ask BellSouth Corporation. My alma mater has been hit with a racial discrimination lawsuit, joining such esteemed victims as The Coca-Cola Company, Lockheed Martin, Home Depot, Georgia Power, and Waffle House.

Five blacks who either work for BellSouth now or did in the past claim the company used "unvalidated tests in a discriminatory manner to deny African-American employees opportunity for advancement." They are seeking class-action status, and guess who their attorneys are? None other than the inestimable Johnnie Cochran and Cyrus Mehri, the legal beagles that soaked Coca-Cola for $192.5 million a couple of years ago and who don't work for minimum wage.

If BellSouth is guilty of anything, it is gross naïveté. The powers that be have operated under the mistaken assumption that doing the right thing is the right thing to do. BellSouth has the record to back up its claims of fairness. The National Association for the Advancement of Colored People gave BellSouth the NAACP Corporate Image Award in 2000. BellSouth's general counsel, Charles Morgan, received the American Corporate Counsel's 2000 Corporate Legal Diversity Award. *Fortune* magazine rates the company one of the 50 Best Companies for Asians, Blacks, and Hispanics. Citizens Funds, an organization that specializes in socially and environmentally correct mutual funds, recognized BellSouth with its Corporate Citizenship Award for Diversity. And, of course, the corporation already has the obligatory diversity officer.

These facts wouldn't lead one to believe that the company requires "qualified African-Americans" to pass an exam that many "Caucasians" don't have to take.

I must confess my ignorance here, though. In my three decades at BellSouth, I never knew we cut Caucasians any slack. As a matter of fact, I never knew we had Caucasians working for us. As the plaintiffs no doubt are aware, Caucasians are by definition people who live in Armenia, Azerbaijan, and Georgia (not the Georgia that has Roopville and Homer, but the one that has Tbilisi and Zugdidi).

I retired from BellSouth a decade ago. About all I know about the company today is that people there wish I would quit writing this column because I frequently beat up on the clueless Public Service Commission. The commission then takes out their frustrations on my old company. Most of the people I worked with are now retired. I'm not even sure what BellSouth does anymore. I go to meetings and listen to the current managers talk about wireless communications and DSL and Latin America and I wonder what ever happened to plain old telephone service. But as much as BellSouth has changed, one thing hasn't: The company was and is color-blind.

I once hired a woman to handle media relations in our Washington office. It was a high-profile job. She was black. To my knowledge, nobody knew, asked, or cared about that fact when I brought her on board. What the company was concerned about was that she do the job she was hired for and do it well. Bad press can quickly get you in the BellSouth doghouse, from which there is no return no matter what your race, gender, sexual preference or astrological sign.

I can predict how the lawsuit will end. BellSouth will cave in and pay out millions of dollars to the plaintiffs and their attorneys not because they are guilty but because they don't need the bad publicity. Johnnie Cochran will hold a press conference and crow about having brought an evil corporation to its knees. He'll pocket more than a few bucks for his trouble and then prepare himself to pounce on the next corporate patsy. And don't forget Jesse Jackson, who will find ample opportunities to march around BellSouth's headquarters chanting nonsense rhymes and trying to get a piece of the action.

The real losers, however, will be minority employees in general because to fair-minded people, this lawsuit looks like a power play by unqualified sluggards who can't hack it in the competitive workplace. Their actions demean the efforts of the many minority employees who have succeeded through hard work and conscientious effort. Sadly, BellSouth's labors to provide a diversified workplace will have been for naught in the court of public opinion.

My old company isn't perfect, but they don't deserve this cheap shot, either.

Dear Roy,
Be a Hero;
Push Ethics Law

Governor Roy Barnes
State Capitol

Dear Governor:

I want to thank you for starting your reelection campaign so early. I figure that the more television commercials you run, the less airtime will be available for all the car dealers who scream and act like nincompoops. You are performing a real public service.

I am puzzled about a couple of things, though. You have an ad that shows you as a child selling fruit on the streets of Austell. I am not sure why we need to know that—not that selling fruit on the streets of Austell isn't a noble endeavor. I just can't figure out what that has to do with being governor. Maybe you are assuring us that your boyhood experience was good preparation for all the fruits and nuts you have to deal with today, like state Senator Charles Walker of Augusta, who is slicker than any banana peel you ever encountered in Austell.

The bigger question, however, is why advertise at all? You are a lock for reelection. The political gods have smiled on you by offering up for sacrifice State School Superintendent Linda Schrenko (Frick), Cobb County Commission Chairman Bill Byrne (Frack) and the author of the much beloved natural gas deregulation legislation, former state Senator Sonny Perdue. How do you keep from giggling when you assess your competition?

With rare exception, you nailed down everything you wanted in your first term, including changing the state flag. I am currently fasting so that I can collect on all the lunches I am going to win from people who bet me that changing the flag would get you defeated. What these folks haven't figured out is that as many people are glad you made the change as there are people who are upset with you, and both groups combined are not as large as the crowd in the middle that doesn't care one way or the other. Politically, changing the flag was a no-brainer.

Your second term should be even easier than the first. Since you can't run for reelection, you can do pretty much whatever you want to do. Therefore, let me offer you a suggestion. (You knew I was going to get around to that, didn't you?) Why don't you spend the next four years showing us that state government operates in the people's interest and not in the interest of professional politicians? I don't ever recall citizens being as turned off by state government as they are today. We feel like we're on the outside looking in at some private party to which we were not invited.

You could change that perception drastically with one simple piece of legislation. Strengthen our ethics laws, which are currently the weakest in the nation. I served on the State Ethics Commission for five years and I know firsthand how little power this group has. About all the commission is empowered to do is to see that public officials properly fill out forms about who has given them money for their political campaigns, and the commission doesn't even have sufficient staff to do that. The state's laissez-faire attitude toward the ethical conduct of public officials only serves to make people even more apathetic toward its government.

The Legislature has no desire to hold themselves and others at the public trough accountable for their wheeling and dealing. That leaves it up to you as a soon-to-be second-termer. You would find enormous support from the citizens of Georgia and from the news media for stronger ethics laws—assuming the legislation was meaningful and tough, and not full of glaring loopholes. No one would dare oppose it. This would be your legacy—the governor who returned government to its rightful owners, the people. You would be a hero and as beloved as Ray Charles.

If that isn't enticement enough, think about this: After you leave office, you could go around the country making speeches about how you engineered the toughest ethics laws in the country. People would pay a lot of money to know how you did it. You could retire a wealthy man and you would never have to worry about going back to the streets of Austell and having to open a fruit stand in order to pay your bills.

Pardon me for saying so, but I think strengthening our ethics laws is a peach of an idea.

Your friend,
Dick

Baseball
on the Verge
of Striking Out

May 27, 2002

It looks like Major League baseball is about to go on strike again. "Work stoppages" in the Bigs are becoming old news as our heroes have walked out on us in 1972, '73, '76, '80, '81, '85, '90 and most recently 1994, when the World Series had to be canceled.

You would hope that the people involved in the game would understand that every time there is a strike, more and more fans are alienated. But listen to that noted philosopher, Braves outfielder Larry Jones.

Jones, better known to his adoring legions as "Chipper," suggested recently that a work stoppage—that's baseball lingo for "strike"—would be "perfect" if it came in August and threatened the playoffs. As for those who shell out their hard-earned bucks to support the game, Chipper says, "There has been talk that another work stoppage would kill the game. I don't see that. There will always be baseball fans." In other words, once a sucker, always a sucker.

The average salary of a major league baseball player today is $2.4 million per year. That's the average. Baseball salaries have increased 126-fold since 1967, while the CPI has increased five-fold in the same period. According to the 2000 U.S. Census, U.S. average annual household income is currently $57,045. Do a little math and you will see that the majority of baseball players make that much in four days. In fact, Larry Jones does even better. The Atlanta Braves are paying him $90 million over the next six years to hit a ball with a stick. He gets his $57,000 in a little less than 36 hours.

Have no sympathy for the owners, either. They plead poverty, but trying to understand their bookkeeping is like trying to understand hieroglyphics. Somehow, they manage to come up with the money to pay exorbitant salaries. In defense of the players, if owners are dumb enough to offer that kind of money, who is going to say "no thanks"?

Fans are the last thing on the mind of Major League baseball right now. The assumption is that when all the parties get over their snits and finger pointing, you will meekly accept the higher costs that will inevitably result from settling the "work stoppage" and once again show up to cheer on the boys of summer. You will pay for baseball's avarice, and the baseball lords think that is the way it should be. Major league ticket prices have gone up steadily since the last strike, and we have every reason to believe that they will continue to increase. The same holds true for the cost of parking, concessions and programs. The Atlanta Braves, who received a $209 million stadium free and clear from the Atlanta Committee for the Olympic Games, have the eighth highest ticket prices in the major leagues. They are not paying for the stadium with all that money. They need it to pay Larry Jones $90 million to hit a ball with a stick.

If Major League baseball gets too expensive for your budget, so what? As long as they can get fat-cat corporate types to buy the luxury boxes and get television networks and advertisers to pay for the privilege of showing half-empty stadiums around the country, baseball says you can take it or lump it.

My fervent prayer is that the greedy owners and the out-of-touch players will stay on strike until everybody totally forgets about baseball and starts doing things like taking walks in the park or playing Scrabble or building houses for Habitat for Humanity. Maybe then, owners and players will have to get real jobs in the real world. Maybe Larry Jones can get hired as a sales clerk at Wal-Mart and then tell everybody that the Christmas shopping season would be a perfect time to have a work stoppage but not to worry because there will always be customers. Maybe Larry Jones would get fired for having a big mouth not connected to his brain.

Ice hockey is the world's dumbest game and has no redeeming social value whatsoever. But at least this nonsport understands that and accepts the fact that if they went on strike, nobody would ever know or care. Baseball is not quite there yet, but one more strike should just about do it. At least, that is what I am hoping.

A Salute to Our Unappreciated Heroes

June 3, 2002

My son, Ken, has just completed his first year as a high school science teacher after 20 years in the business world. His students weren't the only ones to get an education this year.

Thankfully, Ken's rookie year was on a good team. Woodland High School in Bartow County is a fairly new school with a modern physical plant in a progressive county. The teaching staff made him feel welcome, the administration was clear in its expectations of him, and he and the kids seemed to hit it off well. Ken also had his brother-in-law, a veteran high school science teacher in Douglas County, to consult with about those things they forgot to tell him when he received his education degree from Kennesaw State.

Still, the first year was no picnic. As a proud and nervous papa watching anxiously from the sidelines, I came to appreciate firsthand how tough being a public school teacher is. Public education is the most over managed, misunderstood, politicized, and least appreciated profession on God's Green Earth. Everybody talks a good game about wanting to improve public education in Georgia, but where the rubber meets the road, I have decided that teachers teach kids in spite of the obstacles we throw in their path.

The bottom line is that we don't seem to trust our teachers. We don't give them a lot of latitude. We tell them what to teach and how to teach it. The teachers are second-guessed every day by people who couldn't begin to endure what teachers have to put up with in the classroom. We tie teachers' hands when it comes to discipline and make them enforce a bunch of silly rules that are understood only by the people who created them. We don't pay teachers squat and then, to add insult to injury, we make them dig into their own pockets for things like copier paper, workbooks, art supplies and the like. Studies show that teachers shell out between $300 and $400 annually for their classroom needs, although nobody seems to know for sure. Whatever the number, it should be zero.

We encumber teachers with meddling politicians, bureaucratic red tape, social experimentation, lawyers, bored kids and apathetic parents and then expect them to turn out well-educated and well-rounded students like the Mars Candy Company turns out M&M's. No one really goes out of their way to support them.

My son discovered in his initial year of teaching that public school students fall generally into three categories. First are the young people seeking a quality education—usually motivated by parents demanding the best from both the teachers and their children. The good news is that these kids can go toe-to-toe with the best private school students in the state. The bad news is that their number is regretfully small. Still, this group is the one that makes teaching fun.

Then come the students just occupying time and space until the law says they can throw in the towel. They generally come from homes that place no value on education. Little can be done to save this group because they don't want to be saved. They have no vision and no future, and nothing their teachers tell them will change that fact.

By far, the largest group is composed of those kids who could be good students if they made the effort. Some do. Some don't. This group is where teachers earn the little money we pay them and where they experience their highest highs and their lowest lows, trying to reach these young people and make them understand the enormous potential that resides within each one of them. Nothing has been more satisfying to my son than to watch a student who has been on mental cruise control suddenly decide to excel in the classroom. Nothing has caused him greater despair that to see a superior intellect go to waste, most likely because of a lack of interest at home.

Despite all the frustrations the profession offers, this story has a happy ending. Ken is looking forward to his second year as a public school teacher. He knows that he is doing good. He knows that he can make a difference in young lives. He knows teaching will never be easy or financially rewarding, but that doesn't matter. He is now a teacher. To him, that's all that matters.

Mighty Murphy
Just Can't
Get Enough

Georgia House Speaker Tom Murphy, who doesn't have anything better to do with his time, has announced that he is running for reelection to the Georgia House of Representatives. Knock me over with a feather.

Murphy said he made the announcement to squelch rumors that he was waxing up his boogie board and headed for Hawaii or that he was running away to join the circus.

One of the reasons he has decided to go back to the legislature instead of getting a real job, Murphy declares, was because "everywhere I went in Georgia, they have asked me to run again. I have never had as much encouragement to run again in all the times I've run before." The Speaker and I must travel in different circles, which should come as no surprise to regular visitors to this space. Everywhere I go in Georgia, the people I talk to think Murphy is an anachronism or an old-time political boss who runs the state as if it were his personal fiefdom.

Political junkies make a big deal out of the fact that Murphy has been in the legislature since 1961 and has been speaker for 30 years, which makes him the longest-serving presiding officer of a state legislative body in the country. Who cares? The only thing that fact means is that he controls everything that goes on under the Gold Dome as suits his personal whims. Legislators have told me privately that if you cross the Speaker, you can forget ever getting a piece of legislation through the House, no matter how worthy the cause. Republicans could show up buck-naked and he wouldn't recognize them. I don't see where any of that accrues to the benefit of Georgia's citizens. Murphy's style of politics was better suited for the early twentieth century, not the twenty-first.

But why should he retire? He has more power than Superman. He decides what will be law and what won't. He has a group of sycophants made up of legislators, lobbyists and assorted political hangers-on who guffaw every time he grins and swoon every time he speaks. People pay homage to him as if he were the emperor. If you had a job like that, would you want to retire?

Besides, the Speaker says there is a lot still to do before he tools off into the sunset. Despite his best efforts, including the reapportionment purge he spearheaded last year, a few Republicans are running around the Capitol acting like they still belong there. In Murphy's mind, such know-nothings must be dealt with decisively before they start doing silly stuff like effectively representing their constituents. The Georgia High School Association may find itself facing another reclassification of its schools if Bremen loses another football game or debate to one of those prissy private schools in Atlanta. Maybe a relative or two would like to be a superior court judge. Being emperor isn't as easy as it looks.

Murphy almost didn't make it back to the last session. A Republican challenger named Bill Heath nearly cleaned his clock in their west Georgia district two years ago, losing by only 500 votes. At that time, I said the Speaker was "toast." He fired off a letter telling me that he never read my columns but resented my implications. That letter is one of my prized possessions, and I hope one day to ask the Great Man how he knew what I said if he never reads my column.

Even though Heath says he is running again, I have no doubt Murphy will win reelection this time around because he won't be asleep at the switch like he was in 2000. But this may really be his Last Hurrah. West Georgia is experiencing a huge influx of growth as people flee Metro Atlanta or move in from out of state. Many of the newcomers don't know Tom Murphy from Alley Oop. A sizable number weren't even on this earth when he first took office. A lot of them are Republican leaning. The Speaker may make it back this time but sooner rather than later, he is going to be voted out of office if he doesn't step down gracefully and go home.

I giggle every time I think about it: Tom Murphy's power and dominion currently reside in the hands of a bunch of yuppie Republicans. Isn't democracy wonderful?

Dear Jane:
We All Make Mistakes

My sad duty today is to report that Esther "Eppie" Friedman Lederer has passed on. You may have known her better as Ann Landers, the nationally syndicated columnist who gave her loyal followers practical advice on issues ranging from birth control to gun control. She leaves a void that is near impossible to fill. How in the world can we function if we can't bare our innermost secrets to a newspaper columnist in Chicago, who will then share them with 90 million readers?

Admittedly, I am not qualified to dispense wisdom like Ann Landers, but The Lady Who Shares My Name said it certainly wouldn't hurt for me to give it a try. She says it would help me become more sympathetic to people and that I might even learn a little political correctness. Speaking of dispensing wisdom, never argue with a woman who will feed you broccoli at the slightest provocation. So without further ado, let's go to the mailbox.

Dear Dick: I weigh 310 pounds and the airlines want me to buy two tickets before I plop my oversized derriere on their planes. What should I do? *Blimpo in Blackshear*

Dear Blimpo: Walk wherever you are going. You might lose some of the lard you have accumulated, and I won't have to sit next to you on the plane and listen to you wheeze.

Dear Dick: My father was Henry Fonda. My brother is Peter Fonda. My niece is Bridget Fonda, but I prefer to remain anonymous because I am so ashamed of something that I did years ago and something I will always deeply regret. Is there any way that I can ever get this stain off my conscience? *Hanoi Jane Doe*

Dear Ms. Doe: Relax. You are forgiven. You couldn't have known what a goober head Ted Turner was when you married him. If that is the worst thing you have ever done, you are OK in my book.

Dear Dick: I want to be the next governor. I ran a commercial referring to the incumbent as a big rat, and now everybody wants to talk about the commercial and not about the campaign. How can I get the citizens of Georgia to focus on the important issues that confront our state in these trying times? *Sonny from the Senate*

Dear Sonny: That's easy. Remind everyone that you were the author of the much-beloved natural gas deregulation bill while you were in the Legislature. Then everybody will forget about the rat commercial. I guarantee it.

Dear Dick: It is obvious that you have a lot of exclusive information about the political scene in Georgia. Can you share with us where you get your information? *Roy from Austell*

Dear Roy: Please don't tell anybody, but Tom Murphy and I are going steady.

Dear Dick: I recently bought an SUV that goes 150 miles per hour and gets eight miles to the gallon. Recently while gabbing on my cell phone and tailgating some poor slob on the interstate, I noticed a little stick on the steering column. When I touched it, a light blinked. Is there something wrong with my status symbol? *A Self-Important Yuppie Boomer*

Dear Self-Important: It's called a turn signal, but don't worry about learning how to use it. It is very complicated.

Dear Dick: You are a right-wing, homophobic, racist, beer-drinking bigot. I am sick and tired of you criticizing outstanding Democrats like Tom Daschle's lap dog, Max Cleland, and Cynthia (Flap Jaw) McKinney. *Bruce*

Dear Bruce: Can't you tell when I'm teasing? I just say stuff like that to stir people up. I'm really on your side.

Dear Dick: You are a left-wing, communist-sympathizing, Baptist-bashing, martini-sipping sissy. I am sick and tired of you criticizing outstanding Republicans like Linda "Frick" Schrenko and Bill "Frack" Byrne. *Big Al*

Dear Big Al: Can't you tell when I'm teasing? I just say stuff like that to stir people up. I'm really on your side.

Dear Dick: I am so frustrated. The Zionist-controlled press in America criticizes my friends and me constantly and for no good reason. Just because we blow ourselves up—along with buildings, airplanes, ships, buses, vacuum cleaners and a few innocent people—doesn't mean we are naughty people. Any advice on how we can improve our image? *Osama Bin Badd* (not my real name)

Dear Mr. Badd: I have some advice, but I don't think it can be printed here. Why don't you swallow a couple of sticks of dynamite and call me in the morning?

Finally this. *Dear Dick:* My twin sister and I used to write advice columns and now it is just me. Any chance I can interest you in a job? *Abigail Whatshername*

Dear Abby: I thought you would never ask.

Frozen DNA Raises Odd Possibilities

July 8, 2002

The Arab terrorists have made sure we can't live in peace. Now it looks like we can't even die in peace.

Ted Williams, a member of the baseball Hall of Fame, passed away a couple of weeks ago. He was the last major leaguer to hit over .400, finishing the 1941 season at .406. Williams' career with the Boston Red Sox included 521 home runs and a .344 lifetime batting average. Baseball aficionados say his numbers would have been even more impressive had he not lost five years serving in World War II and the Korean War. Williams was an extraordinary talent. The slugger claimed his eyesight was so keen that he could see the strings of the baseball coming toward him at upwards of 90 mph. Truly, we will never see his likes again. Or will we?

His children have been in a heated dispute, so to speak, over whether or not to freeze Ted Williams and sell his DNA at some time in the future. His daughter strongly expressed her opposition, saying it was "immoral." His son, an entrepreneur if there ever was one, proposed that if they couldn't freeze the whole body, maybe they could just freeze Daddy's head. I don't understand how all of this works, but I think the son reasons that the old man's DNA could be sold to the highest bidder who I assume could then use it to make a person who could hit .400 anytime he or she wanted.

I haven't checked with my own kids, but I have a strong feeling that saving my DNA is not a hot topic of conversation between them. I suspect they both shudder to think of someone walking around this earth in the future acting like their father. The future Dick Yarbrough-type person would be easy to recognize—getting lost every time they went to Macon and always paying full price for anything they bought one day before the newspaper ran ads announcing a half-price sale.

There is another reason not to freeze me or my head. My head and I despise the cold. Ever since we attended the Winter Olympics in Lillehammer, Norway, the two of us have developed a strong aversion to snow, ice, wind, frozen ears, runny noses and having to wear three coats and four pair of gloves to breakfast.

Don't get me wrong. I'm not saying that freezing somebody's DNA doesn't merit further study. Some people are probably worth a second visit. We could use all the Mother Teresas we could manufacture. Same with Billy Graham and Thomas Jefferson and Nelson Mandela and Vince Dooley. But you can bet your last molecule that if we can duplicate these outstanding individuals, somebody will figure out how to create another Saddam Hussein or Eminem or the goofy judges of the Ninth Circuit Court of Appeals. Copying these people doesn't sound like much progress to me and it sure isn't worth getting yourself frozen and coming back to see them go through their acts again.

On the other hand, maybe the smart folks who know about all this stuff could greatly improve the original product. Maybe instead of hitting .400 all the time, a future Ted Williams could hit .600 and not only see the strings on the baseball but take a quick snooze while waiting for the ball to get to the plate. Maybe we could whip up a new version of House Speaker Tom Murphy who would agree to wear a seat belt when driving, like the rest of us mortals. Maybe we could clone a kinder, gentler Ted Turner, which would probably necessitate the new model having its jaw permanently wired shut. If we could keep ol' Looney Tunes quiet, we might even consider making another patriotic statesperson like the Right Honorable Cynthia McKinney, the pride and joy of Georgia's Fourth district, although right offhand I can't think why we would want to do that, even if we could.

Let me state this clearly for the record. I am unalterably opposed to the notion of freezing the deceased and using their DNA. However, if somebody offered to make me a couple of Marilyn Monroes on a trial basis, I would certainly be willing to reconsider my position. And she wouldn't even have to hit .400.

One More Thing About That Pledge Edict

Pardon me if I go back over ground that I plowed a couple of weeks ago, but based on the mail I have received, some more thoughts may be in order about the recent 9th Circuit Court of Appeals ruling on the Pledge of Allegiance.

As you will recall, Michael Newdow, an atheist from California, went to court to have the Pledge of Allegiance declared unconstitutional in the public schools because it contains the dreaded words, "under (You-Know-Who)." Mr. Newdow believes that saying this pledge in public schools violates the church-state separation concept. Why? Because the schools are supported by taxpayers' dollars. Incidentally, those dollars include the words "In (You-Know-Who) We Trust," which would seem to be an even more egregious attack on Mr. Newdow's deeply held principles, but, hey, you can only attack "You-Know-Who" one bite at a time.

Most people I heard from were incensed by the court's decision. We, the People, are frightened, angry and frustrated. We saw Arab terrorists kill thousands of innocent people on national television for no reason other than the victims happened to live in a country that many Arabs despise. We heard our president vow revenge for the senseless murders, and yet ten months later we can't be certain that Osama bin Laden isn't sitting in some cave somewhere planning another round of terror.

More than anything else in these dark days we want security and peace of mind. Most of us find that comfort in a Higher Being, whether a small minority likes it or not. Now a federal court of Appeals, which is so suspect that it would likely declare the bald eagle unconstitutional because it discriminates against people of hair, decides to boot the Pledge of Allegiance out of our schools. That decision was more than we are willing to accept. A recent *Newsweek* poll says that 87 percent of Americans don't want the pledge changed. Therefore, the pledge isn't going to be changed. We, the People, have spoken.

Some of those people writing to defend the court's ruling couldn't wait to exclaim "Gotcha!" by reminding me that the words "under (You-Know-Who)" were placed in the Pledge of Allegiance in 1954. Obviously, they didn't take time to look at the picture that accompanies this column, although I am flattered if they thought I was a gleam in my father's eye in 1954. I was of voting age when the phrase was added. I remember that action being taken because we were as frightened of the Russians then as we are the Arabs today. Hence, we appealed to a Higher Being to help us through the hard times. When the going gets tough, we seem to realize that we aren't the highest power.

Other writers claim that the Declaration of Independence does not mention God. I see the terms "the laws of Nature and of Nature's God" and "endowed by their Creator" and "protection of divine Providence" and wonder what Declaration of Independence they are reading.

A Californian wrote me to say this nation is not a democracy; it is a republic. The writer says "a true democracy affords no protection for the minority viewpoint from majority rule—whereas our constitution wisely affords certain protections (the Bill of Rights) to all citizens, regardless of what the majority think." The writer is dealing in semantics. A republic is defined as "a government in which supreme power resides in a body of citizens entitled to vote and is exercised by elected officers and representatives responsible to them and governing according to law." We, the People, exercise that supreme power, not the courts or any single individual. Our elected representatives express our will. That is why our republic is a democracy.

But enough of this. The Pledge of Allegiance is going to stay as is. Let us move on to more pressing issues. Business is cooking its books. Larry Jones isn't hitting squat for the Atlanta Braves. California has passed Claxton, Georgia, as the fruitcake capital of the world, and I still can't get the squirrels out of my birdfeeders. I hereby declare I will waste no more ink on Mr. Newdow and his ignoble cause. I'll let You-Know-Who deal with him. It couldn't happen to a more deserving person.

Recent News
Provides
Knee-Slappers

The Lady Who Shares My Name got right to the point: "Stop sounding like all the other media fussbudgets in the country and write something funny for a change." Her opinion is that we are all in a funk because we are worried about a bunch of Middle East lowlifes blowing up everything we cherish (the bad news) along with themselves (the good news). She doesn't think being a cranky old man is helping anybody's mood.

Besides, she says, everybody who peruses this space already knows that I think Ted Turner is nuttier than all the goober plants in Georgia; that ice hockey is the world's dumbest game and has no redeeming social value; that gas-guzzling SUVs ought to be banned from our roads along with the yuppie-boomers who drive them at supersonic speeds; and that Baptists believe we will all go to hell if (gasp!) women are allowed to become preachers.

"Leave these poor souls alone for awhile," the Lady instructed, "and make us laugh." No way I will argue with her because when I do, she feeds me broccoli. But I'm not in a funny mood these days. The only joke that comes immediately to mind is the Ambassador to Outer Space, Congressperson Cynthia McKinney, of Georgia's Fourth District. She is about to get a bad case of tendinitis from patting herself on the back. When it was revealed that vague warnings about terrorist attacks had been coming into the White House since 1995, she and her mindless supporters claim this proved her charges about deliberate neglect by the Bush administration to the warnings. She insinuated that the president's father and others in the defense industry would benefit financially from a war, so George Bush looked the other way. Nothing has come to light that exonerates her or her babbling. Sorry, Madame Flapjaw. Your conspiracy theory is still my favorite joke.

I'll admit that I consider the latest developments in Sonny Perdue's well-oiled campaign for governor pretty funny also. Evidently, the same wise souls who urged him to champion natural gas deregulation legislation when he was in the State Senate have convinced Perdue that a classy advertising campaign depicting Governor Roy Barnes as a big rat would make a lot of people from across the state rush out and enthusiastically support the Republican from Bonaire. Alas, the only group that has openly endorsed the campaign to date is the Georgia Association of Rat Breeders and Gerbil Enthusiasts (GARBAGE).

And I had to stifle a giggle at the will-he-won't-he speculation over House Speaker Tom Murphy's decision to run again and grace us with his benevolent leadership. To the political pundits who are suffering serious hyperventilation awaiting word from the Bremen Brahman, I'll let you in on a little late-breaking news. Most folks I talk to don't give a rip one way or the other. They think Murphy is about seven centuries behind the times and is Exhibit A on why so many people are turned off by their state government. And that's no joke.

I chuckled when I heard that Barbara Dooley had announced she will be a Republican candidate for the new Twelfth Congressional District seat, which runs from somewhere east of Hartford, Connecticut, to Key West, Florida. The Democrats had custom-tailored the district for Charles "Champ" Walker, son of State Senator Charles Walker, the Kingfish of Augusta. (Not to be critical, but when my son came of age I gave him a bicycle.) Now, Barbara is threatening to crash the Democrats' private party. Her chances of winning are slim, but she'll make the race a lot of fun.

Finally, a group of al-Qaida terrorists are creeping through the desert when they hear somebody holler from behind a sand dune: "One good ol' boy from Georgia can whup a hundred Al Queda." Furious, the commander sends his 100 best men over the dune and a fight commences. After a few minutes, there is silence.

The good ol' boy calls out again. "Ain't you got no better fighters than that?" The enraged commander sends another thousand men over the dune with rockets and machine guns. Another battle ensues. Then more silence.

Eventually, one mortally wounded Al Queda fighter crawls back over the dune and pleads with his commander, "Don't send any more men. It's a trap. There's two of them!"

Now, that's funny.

Zapping Trash on TV's Wasteland

August 5, 2002

Recently, a bunch of television critics—people who are paid to watch television and who make sportswriters look almost relevant—gathered together with network executives to discuss the current state of the television business. The big issue was not the garbage that networks serve us daily, but the fact that you and I are growing tired of all the advertising clutter on television and are find ways to avoid it. The critics and poobahs need not worry. As bad as television commercials are, they are better than most of today's network programs, unless you enjoy watching people eat worms on a dare, as I witnessed recently on one of the networks.

Devices are now being manufactured that will automatically zap commercials so that we can watch the few minutes of programming the networks allow between ads. This development is a major trauma to television networks. Most of their revenue comes from sponsors, and they don't want us to omit the commercials. Otherwise, advertisers won't underwrite important cultural fare, like people eating worms on a dare.

One television mogul, Jamie Kellner, who is president of Turner Broadcasting, a division of AOL/Time Warner/Ted Turner/Looney Tunes, predicted that if we keep zapping commercials then we are going to have to pay $250 a year more just to have the privilege of watching a bunch of air-headed, tattooed blond girls get pregnant. Perish the thought.

"Not so fast," says Leslie Moonves, president of CBS. Moonves insists the commercial-zapping machines haven't taken over the world yet and, besides, he has an alternative to commercials—product placement. Instead of enduring Screaming Dan the New Car Man prattling at you every fifteen minutes or so to buy his gas-guzzling SUVs, you might see Morley Safer pick up a bar of Ivory soap during "60 Minutes" and slyly set it in camera range in a way that will make you want to run out and buy a case or two. But product placement does have some drawbacks. Advertisers might object to associating with certain shows. Moonves cites his own network's blood-and-guts show *CSI* as an example. "How do you do an autopsy and have a diet Coke next to it?" Are network presidents heavy thinkers or what?

Personally, I think the television industry is way behind the learning curve on this issue. I have been zapping commercials for years, and I don't require a complicated technological gizmo. All I need is my handy remote control with a mute button. I zap ads that feature rap music (which is most of them) or any that have cats in them, and I zap all commercials that show some white guy as a befuddled jerk being set straight by his superior-acting wife and smirked at by his kids. Advertisers do this to white guys because if they made blacks or Asians or women look that stupid, they'd receive a corporate butt-kicking from all the special-interest groups. White guys have no special-interest groups to defend them, unless you count the Republican Party. But Republicans are too busy fighting with each other these days to have the time to take up for white guys.

I zap political ads because they insult even my limited intelligence, especially the one featuring Zell Miller talking about Max Cleland's leadership in the Senate. I assume Miller had his fingers crossed when he made that commercial, because surely he doesn't mean it.

I not only zap commercials, but I also zap people I don't like. It has been years since Jesse Jackson, Ted Kennedy, Phil Donahue, Jerry Falwell, Yasser Arafat, talent-challenged Alex Baldwin, or anyone associated with Atlanta's Concerned Black Clergy has uttered a word on the television sets in my home, and as long as my remote control holds out, they never will.

Although it fries the hide of a couple of journalism professors I know, I am glad I write a newspaper column. I don't have to pause in the middle of a great thought to accommodate Screaming Dan, the New Car Man. The mute button is rendered powerless against me. I don't have to hold up a bar of Ivory soap while you read this. Best of all, I don't have to eat worms on a dare or associate with anyone who does.

9/11 a Year Later: Disappointment Reigns

We are approaching the first anniversary of the Arab terrorists attacks on the World Trade Center and the Pentagon. In the next couple of weeks, you are going to be swamped by a tidal wave of commentary, analysis, soul-searching, pontificating and second-guessing by those of us who have opinions and are paid to subject you to them.

If I wait to say my piece, my thoughts will become lost in the cacophony. If I say it now, you will have the benefit of one man's opinion and I will feel better for having gotten some things off my chest.

I still can't look at pictures of the airplanes crashing into the twin towers without feeling ill. That there are people so demented that they think cowardly acts are heroic is incomprehensible in what is supposed to be a civilized world. Many people would celebrate the deaths of thousands of innocent people by staging celebrations and burning American flags shows that much of our world is still uncivilized.

I am disappointed in our government. We should have retaliated before the smoke cleared on Sept. 11. Is the most powerful nation on earth capable of punishing those who kill American people on American soil, or are we too worried about our image in the world? Even the terrorists must be surprised at our lack of action.

I am disappointed that those people who perpetrated this evil act and those who supported them show little or no remorse. For some reason, our government feels compelled to assure Saudi Arabia that we don't hold them liable for anything that happened. The Saudis have responded by refusing to allow us to use their airbases in case we attack the terrorist state of Iraq and by holding telethons for the families of the terrorists. Some friends.

Speaking of friends, we have none. The sooner we understand that, the better. There is no question that Iraq is developing weapons of mass destruction intended for use in the United States but our allies in Europe, who wouldn't be here today if not for our aid after World War II, won't lift a hand to help us. We are going to have to go it alone and to hell with what the rest of the world thinks.

About the only good news to come this past year is that self-described comedian Bill Maher was kicked off the air after informing the plebeians that the terrorists were "courageous." His departure wasn't a freedom of speech issue as some claim. We were so disgusted by his smugness and arrogance that we threatened his network and his sponsors, who promptly deserted him. Gay rights groups have been employing this tactic for years. It was about time we plebeians learned to use it, too.

Since the attacks, we have had to wrestle with the question of how to increase our security without losing our individual freedoms. To date, we haven't found the answer. The much-vaunted Department of Homeland Security has the look of a bumbling, ineffective federal bureaucracy. The idea of suggesting that ordinary citizens and delivery people act as spies and snitches gives me the shudders. So do civil libertarians, who stick their heads in the sand and act as if nothing unusual has happened.

The news media have shown over the past twelve months that we could do with a little soul-searching of our own. Are we really neutral observers like sportswriters at a prizefight, or do we have a stake in the outcome? Do we have an obligation to publish leaked war plans and possibly endanger those charged with the execution of those plans? Do we understand that the First Amendment will apply only if we remain free? Journalists need to remember that we are Americans first, media people second.

Of all that has happened to us, the biggest tragedy is that my children and grandchildren will never know the security that I have enjoyed. Suicide bombers and technological and biological terror will become a way of life. Your family and mine have done nothing to deserve this. That is why I am so unforgiving of those involved directly or indirectly in the attacks last September.

I wish I could be optimistic about the future, but I'm not sure where we are headed or how we are going to get there. I just wish we didn't have to make the trip.

Farewell Dear Cynthia: The Problem Was Y-O-U

August 26, 2002

Honorable Cynthia McKinney
Somewhere in Outer Space

I apologize for bothering you at this awkward time, but I wanted you to know that I am here to offer my support in these difficult days. It is the least I can do. You have provided so much fodder for this column over the past several years that I owe you, big-time.

I am going to miss your outrageous behavior and your off-the-wall comments. I am going to miss the annual ritual of watching you try to hug the president on national television before every State of the Union speech. Seeing you elbow your colleagues to get to the aisle and smile that loopy smile of yours as the president walked by became a tradition in our home, like watching the Rose Parade. You became an important part of my life. I always knew that when I grew tired of picking on Ted Turner or proponents of the old state flag, I could count on your doing something totally bizarre that would be worth a column or two.

Perhaps a good place to start would be to offer an in-depth analysis of your recent defeat in the Fourth Congressional District at the hands of Judge Denise Majette. Your father, Representative Billy McKinney, said on television that the problem was "J-E-W." While it is difficult to disagree with someone who built his reputation fostering racial harmony as your Dad has (remember when he called your opponent in your last election a "racist Jew"?) I would offer an alternative theory: The problem was "Y-O-U." The voters were tired of you and your mouth.

Blaming your defeat on Republicans crossing over and voting against you is easy, but that theory won't fly. If you look at how well the GOP has fared in Georgia over the years, you are giving them much more credit than they deserve. This crowd enjoys fighting with each other too much to worry about what Democrats are doing. You got beat because you lost touch with your constituents. You got beat because you assumed that black people are monolithic and think and act in lockstep. That outlook is not only wrong, it is insulting. The people told you so with their votes.

You got beat because you forget the advice of the late Speaker of the House Tip O'Neill, who said, "All politics is local." Despite a lapse in grammar, his admonition was right on. Your constituents weren't impressed with your opinions on the Middle East – most of which were wrong anyway. Your conspiracy theory that the White House promoted war just to enrich the defense industry was way past nutty. Obviously, they weren't impressed when you paraded Jesse Jackson and Louis Farrakahn around the district just before the election, as if they had something substantive to contribute to the campaign. Your constituents wanted somebody in your office to return their calls and answer their letters and for you to come home on the weekend and shake their hands and find out what was on their minds. You ignored them because you were too busy trying to be a national figure. If that nation was Saudi Arabia, you may have succeeded.

Just as whites booted out the abrasive Bob Barr in favor of low-key John Linder, blacks decided that your grandstanding style of politics didn't fit their needs anymore – if it ever did. Your constituents want an effective representative, not a showboating publicity hound.

Now that your political career is in the dumper, you say you may go back to school and finish work on your Ph.D. Good for you. Most of the important stuff to learn, though, doesn't appear in the textbooks. Perhaps the most important lesson I gleaned from my college experience came from one of the most influential professors in my life, Dr. Raymond Cook. One day during my freshman year, I stood up in his literature class and offered my opinions on a particular poem, providing clear evidence that I had no idea what I was talking about. Dr. Cook scolded me severely in front of the class. Then he pointed his finger at me and said, "Mr. Yarbrough, always think before you speak." I never forgot that. Dr. Cook's advice saved my career more than once. I have the feeling, Representative McKinney, that it could have saved yours, too.

Your humble scribe,
Dick Yarbrough

Cops Have the Most Thankless Job

September 8, 2002

There is one trait common to all humankind. No matter our age, IQ or political leanings, we all secretly consider ourselves experts when it comes to the other person's job. It doesn't matter if we aren't competent at our own work. We watch what other people do and know in our hearts we could do it better.

One of the toughest and most thankless jobs in America is law enforcement. There is no way I could ever be a police officer and, I suspect, neither could most of the rest of us. But we sure as hell can second-guess everything the police do, forgetting that sometimes they have a split-second to make a decision and we have weeks to critique their actions from the safety of the sidelines.

Law enforcement is equal parts mind-numbing tedium and mind-blowing terror. When an officer leaves for work, his or her family has no way of knowing if there will be a next meal together. A couple of weeks ago, a Carroll County deputy sheriff got up from the dinner table to assist in the chase of an arson suspect. He was shot to death for his efforts.

We don't care about the police until we need them. If we find ourselves threatened we want them to protect us, no matter what the risks. Other than that, leave us alone. We resent being told what to do. It impinges on our personal liberty. Let us speed, run red lights and tailgate while we yak away on our car phones. If we are stopped, give us the opportunity to lie or cajole our way out of a traffic citation so that we can laugh about the experience to our friends and then burn up the roads again. Otherwise, we may get downright hostile.

When I lived in East Point, the local judge received a call from an irate citizen who had been stopped for running a red light and wanted to complain about the officer's curt manner. "Do you know where he had been before he stopped you?" the judge asked. "He had just told a family their child had been killed after running a stop sign. Maybe this officer saved your life."

A South Georgia sheriff recently told me about a prominent citizen who was livid over the attitude of the deputy that had stopped her for a moving violation. What she didn't know was that the officer's car had a video camera. A review of the tape showed that the deputy had handled the stop exactly as he was supposed to do, including showing her more courtesy than she had shown him. Last I heard, the sheriff was trying to get the complainant and her husband to review the tape with him and point out the source of their complaint. Good for him.

Are there bad police officers? Absolutely. Are there police officers that abuse their authority? Certainly. There are also bad teachers and preachers and doctors and lawyers. And don't forget the CEOs and accountants that abused their authority and ruined the lives of a lot of people in the process.

The truth is that police officers are no worse than the rest of society and probably better than most of it. It continues to amaze me that we can find people willing to put up with all the verbal and physical abuse, the criticism, a lack of appreciation for what they do and the very real possibility that somebody may kill them before they can ever collect their meager pension.

I have never gotten a ticket in the half century I have had a driver's license. That doesn't guarantee that I won't get one in the future. The most likely opportunity will be when I haul a tailgating truck driver out of his cab and kick his rear end into the next time zone. I know that is wrong, but so is tailgating.

No doubt I will huff and puff and wonder why the police couldn't better spend their time stopping all the crazy drivers on the road, instead of upstanding citizens like me. If I do, I should re-read this column, particularly the part about the East Point judge, and understand that some unappreciated souls may have saved my life, whether I wanted them to or not. I just hope I remember to thank them.

A Few Questions Without Ready Answers

September 1, 2002

Some days I find I have more questions than answers, an admission sure to amaze my friends and confound my enemies.

For example, why did only one in four eligible voters take time to cast their ballots in the September primary in Georgia? This dismal record is nothing new for us. According to Secretary of State Cathy Cox's office, never in our state's history have more than 50 percent of eligible citizens participated in an election. There should be a law that says if you don't vote, you are forbidden to gripe about anything the government does. Violators would be forced to watch all of Jerry Lewis' old movies. I suspect that some do-gooder from the ACLU would immediately have the law overturned, saying it infringes on our You-Know-Who-given right to thumb our noses at our civic responsibilities.

Why didn't black preachers in Atlanta like Joseph Lowery and Tim McDonald criticize Rep. Billy McKinney for slandering Jews during his loopy daughter Cynthia's failed bid for reelection to Congress? They yammered incessantly about former Atlanta Braves John Rocker's ill-stated comments a couple of years ago, but not a peep from either of them after McKinney's diatribes. Could it be they condone racial epithets from their own people, but not from others? Do they understand what a disservice they do to the ministry by their hypocrisy? Do they care?

Is Senator Max Cleland's record so abysmal that ultra-popular Senator Zell Miller has to shill for him? I have seen more of Miller defending Cleland's record over the past month that I have seen of Cleland. If he has done such a great job in his six years in the Senate, why does Cleland have to send Miller to tell us about it? Will Republican challenger Saxby Chambliss remember to ask Cleland that question?

At a time when Arab nations hold us hostage to their oil, why do American automobile manufacturers insist on producing gas guzzlers like the Cadillac Escalade (12 mpg), the Ford Expedition

(12-15 mpg) and the GMC Yukon (12-14 mpg)? And why do we buy them? Whose side are we on?

Remember Adolf Hitler? If not, read up on him. He was a madman who built a fanatical following among the German people. Much of the world, including the United States, spent several years trying to appease Hitler or ignore him. As a result, more than 20 million people lost their lives in World War II. Four hundred thousand were Americans. Today, we have another madman named Saddam Hussein on the loose, and the world is trying to appease him or ignore him. This time the results could be even worse. Do we ever learn anything?

Would Georgia rank last in the country in SAT scores if we kicked the politicians and the lawyers and the social scientists out of the state's educational system and let teachers teach? As a bonus, why not give teachers the right to tan the fannies of some of the smart-mouthed kids they have to endure? Trying couldn't hurt. Whatever we are doing now doesn't seem to be working.

Why are our politicians loath to strengthen the state's ethics laws, which are among the weakest in the nation? Word among political observers is that House Speaker Tom Murphy won't support Governor Roy Barnes' proposal to put some teeth into the law—something the governor should have done four years ago—and give the public the confidence that our elected officials are free of conflicts of interest. Why would Tom Murphy not support ethics reform? Who elected him king? Does he understand that this kind of arrogance further alienates the people of the state from their government and gives us another excuse not to vote? Why doesn't Murphy retire?

Do we really care that politicians thumb their noses at us? Are we going to let race-mongers like Billy McKinney continue to feed at the public trough? Are we going to keep driving gas-guzzlers and thereby remain hostage to Arab oil? Will we ignore Saddam Hussein, hoping he just goes away? Are we going to demand that our public schools improve? Do we care enough about anything to get off our duff and vote this November?

I've got a lot more questions, but my head hurts. I like the world better when I have all the answers. Don't you?